Improving
Personal Relationships

Improving
Personal Relationships

by Marta Merajver-Kurlat

Jorge Pinto Books Inc.
New York

Published by Jorge Pinto Books Inc., website: www.pintobooks.com
Cover design © 2009 by Nigel Holmes, website: www.nigelholmes.com
Book design by Charles King, website: www.ckmm.com

ISBN 978-1-934978-24-5
1-934978-24-8

BIBLIOTREATMENT SERIES

This book is not intended as a replacement for professional medical, dietary, financial, or psychiatric assistance, if that is needed.

Contents

Note: the worksheets in this book can be downloaded in 8½×11 format:

http://www.pintobooks.com/images/relationships_worksheets.pdf

Acknowledgements

I wish to thank publisher Jorge Pinto for his invaluable assistance throughout the writing process of this book. He closely followed the development and treatment of the issues discussed, making most useful suggestions and comments and offering his enthusiastic encouragement at difficult moments. The *Bibliotreatment* series is very much his child and I am deeply grateful to him for entrusting me with the task of raising such a child.

M.M.K.

Introduction

For reasons unknown to me, lots of people love being lied to despite strong assertions to the contrary. I guess that they find comfort when told that the formula for love, health, success, and happiness lies within their reach. The only thing they need do, according to some gurus of the day, is think hard enough of what they want to accomplish while dismissing all negative ideas, for these will attract the very evils people fear so much.

Other gurus promise exactly the same benefits if only you will exercise your mind in order to slough off your old self and be metaphorically reborn "as a different person." Still others claim that you should begin thinking in a completely different way, and another group posits that your emotions, not your thoughts need a makeover.

The phrase "the gurus of the day" clearly speaks of the fact that present gurus have replaced a past generation of solution whizzes, and that they will in turn be replaced by a fresh litter of "enlightened winners" in a relatively short time.

In short, gurus come and go, yet human problems stay unless some other path is chosen to solve what can be solved and cope with what cannot. The "recipes" offered in guru style seem to appeal to magic thought, which is natural in children up till six years of age, but highly dangerous in adults. Why dangerous? Because one disappointment after another brings about bitterness, distrust, and a deeply embedded belief that you are ruled by fate, or that you're an inborn loser. Thus your self-esteem drops to the lowest levels possible, and you acquire a beautiful, self-fulfilled prophecy at the cost of countless attempts to follow this or that course.

Many years ago, Dr. Robert Schwartz wrote an amazing book called *Diets Don't Work*, and in the late nineties he strengthened his views on the subject by publishing a sequel entitled *Diets Still Don't Work*. Paraphrasing Schwartz, I am telling you straight away that "methods to achieve happiness don't work." They don't for the simple reason that people are unique, and it is quite impossible to impose uniformity of thought, feeling, and lifestyle on every human being. The metaphor underlying Ira Levin's *The Stepford Wives* may well act as a warning of the price one would pay for the sake of uniformity. You could ask what's wrong with everyone wanting unblemished happiness. Nothing indeed, once you accept that "happiness" and "well being" don't mean the same to everyone. You have every right to seek whatever you think will make you happy as long as you don't deny your most precious treasure: your uniqueness.

I am therefore not making any promises or predictions about the degree of well being you will reach in your interactions with others. I am definitely not a guru nor do I intend to be mistaken for one. I am just offering you tools to look into yourself and into others in the hope that they will help you improve discomfiting aspects of your life.

This book is then an invitation to explore the various types of personal relationships we enter into along with what makes them positive and enriching. While it is true that some of our relationships are more meaningful to us than are others, *all* relationships, if properly handled, may broaden our minds and contribute to our well being.

Nevertheless, we sometimes relate to the wrong people or to the right people in the wrong way. By the "wrong people" I mean those who use us as a means to an end. We need to learn how to identify and avoid them without enacting negative feelings towards them. In most cases, these people do not consciously intend to harm us, though their unconscious world—*who* they are—somehow drives them to ill-treat others. The danger lies not in overt hostility, for this we can promptly recognize, but in the subtle ways in which ill treatment can work.

There is a possibility that you yourself may unknowingly belong in this group. Thus it will be interesting as well as enlightening to learn how you relate to others. Regardless of where you stand now as far as relationships go, perhaps you will see fit to change your approach to other people and to yourself.

You may wonder, "why to myself?" Simply because the first personal relationship in which you need to succeed is with yourself. This means that you need to know yourself, as has been amply discussed in *Living with Stress*, the first book of this series. Without awareness of who you really are, what you really want, and what you believe you want yet unconsciously reject, you may engage in empty, disappointing relationships. Your relationship with yourself is the model on which your relationship with everyone else is shaped.

Our contact with others is ruled by the interplay between

our personal traits and environmental factors. People seem to enjoy more fulfilling relationships in small towns than in big cities. The pace of the town is slower, and the phenomenon of external time versus internal time is best exemplified in small town versus big city.

External time is the same for everybody. It is measured by clocks and watches, and has a fixed duration wherever you are. Conversely, internal time is entirely dependent on how you feel about what you are doing at a given moment. When you are bored, for example, you might say that time "drags on." On the other hand, when you fill your days and evenings with commitments you can hardly cope with or with enjoyable activities, you probably complain that time "flies." Having "no time" is solely an effect of our perception.

Unhampered by externally or internally imposed pressures, the dwellers of small towns perform their daily duties and cultivate relationships. This is something to bear in mind: relationships do not bloom like wild flowers. They need care and tending or else they whither and die, leaving us angry, sad, frustrated, and mistrustful of others and ourselves.

In contrast, city dwellers tend to rush from morning to night, too absorbed in material concerns to make room for others in their hectic lives. How many working parents sit down to breakfast with their children in the city? How many childless couples, briefcase in hand, gulp down a cup of coffee standing by the kitchen board and take leave of each other until the evening reunites them in a state of exhaustion? How often are we there for a friend or relative who needs us today, without having scheduled a meeting in "plenty of time"?

Am I saying that we are responsible for the kind of relationships we engage in? Yes, at least as regards our role in them. We are certainly not accountable for other people's behavior; however, changes in our attitude and clear communication of our feelings may induce great positive changes in those we relate to. Even occasional or casual relationships may be sources of pleasure and well being, although we are naturally more interested in enhancing lasting personal bonds. What you need to bear in mind is that in the journey of life some relationships are "stations," while others will become indispensable companions that will walk with you all the way. Who these will be depends mostly on a Biblical commandment that tends to be misunderstood: "Love thy neighbor as thyself." The emphasis lies on "thyself." You must love yourself first, or else you will be incapable of loving others. With exceptions that we will discuss, love breeds love. Ultimately, fulfilling relationships rest on different kinds of love. One human tragedy is the belief that love, though expressed differently by different people, amounts to a universal feeling. Let us then start our own journey by trying to define a notion that seems to have lost meaningfulness insofar as we all think that it is self-explanatory.

1

Your Relationship with Yourself

All you need is love
—Lennon & McCartney

Yes, all you need is love, once you have made up your mind about what you believe love means. In this chapter we'll try to reach some sort of consensus with which you feel comfortable. On the other hand, you need to know right from the start that the love you need the most, once your love patterns have been established, is not the one you receive but the one you are able to give. The epigraph to this chapter can be read both ways, only giving turns out to be much more difficult than receiving.

Love has no genetic inscription. It must be learned, though not from books. We first begin to recognize love in a rather hazy way as infants. What our parental figures do in order to make us feel physically and emotionally protected are object lessons in love. Parental figures are not necessarily mothers or fathers. In the infant's mind, anybody who raises her as a parent takes on the role of a parent.

Unfortunately, not all parental figures are role models in matters of love. Still, assuming that those who raise us know how to love us, at some point in our early development we instinctively want to repay them with something we think will make them happy. This is the first step towards grasping a feeling for which individual explanations will differ widely on account of our uniqueness.

Erich Fromm (1900-1980) was an outstanding psychoanalyst and philosopher to whose thought I shall often resort in order to set down some clues that may be of help. Fromm says that, regardless of individual variations, all forms of love share four basic elements: **care, responsibility, respect**, and **knowledge**.

Before elucidating how these elements relate to personal relationships, you need to become aware that, first and foremost, you need to apply them to you. He who cannot love himself will certainly not love anyone else, even if he is convinced to the contrary.

There are a thousand ways in which you can take **care** of and care for yourself. You are made up of a soul and a body. Both need to be tended to in equal measure. Besides religious comfort, which does not seem to be available to everyone, the soul can be nurtured by beauty. I certainly do not mean the beauty of what money can buy. It is precisely what you cannot buy—and therefore cannot sell—that will fill your soul with wonder at the gifts of Nature. Sunrise and sunset, an endless variety of landscapes, the changing colors of the sky parade before your eyes if only you make a conscious effort to look about. The work of men and women who devoted their life to producing beauty is also yours through the arts. It is not necessary to possess an artwork, but to let it into your soul so that it will become a part of you. Why such insistence on the appreciation of beauty? Because physics does not allow for a void, unless beauty becomes a constituent part of your soul, it will grab at ugliness disguised as one or all of the cardinal sins. Greed, envy, lust, gluttony, pride, wrath, and sloth are independent of whether you are a believer or an atheist. Even if you do not regard them as "sins," they poison the soul, and eventually spread their deadly fumes onto others. Care of the soul through the apprehension of beauty makes you a better person, and you are the first beneficiary of your own kind soul.

What about your body? Many people neglect and harm it in incredible ways. Let us assume that you don't deny your body the advantages of soap and water, which works fine for the "wrapping," for what you and others can see. Still, one non-psychological definition maintains that you are what you eat. The emphasis is on "what," for you already know that's not *who* you are. I would say that you are also what you do to your body. If you stuff yourself with junk food, or skip meals, or starve yourself in the hope that you will end up resembling a fashion model, or unnecessarily use prescribed drugs, or indulge in the so-called recreational drugs, or do not exercise, or exercise to exhaustion, you are slowly destroying your body. You see then that self-care goes far beyond your daily shower/s.

Write down truthfully how you take care of your soul and body on the blank page/s at the end of this chapter.

3

Fromm draws on the etymology of the word **respon-sibility,** and says that "responsibility, in its true sense, is [...] my response to the needs, expressed or unexpressed, of another human being."[1]

The last phrase of the quote makes perfect sense because the author was not speaking about self-love. However, I am, so I will reword it to refer to the psychic needs of an individual who needs to find out the extent to which she loves herself. One word of warning: self-love is not syn-onymous with selfishness. A selfish person is self-centered, cares about nobody but herself, wants to possess everything and everyone she fancies, and her utmost pleasure is grab-bing, accumulating, shutting out others from her private treasure. As a consequence, the selfish person, trapped in emotional starvation (for she soon despises what she has and craves for the "greener grass" lying beyond), lives in constant frustration. Paradoxically, the selfish person hates herself because she cannot give herself full satisfaction. In other words, she cannot love herself.

Going back to our needs, rather than voicing them to ourselves, we think about them. From this point of view, our needs, those that no one but us can fulfill, are known to ourselves only. What exactly are psychic needs? According to the experts and widely speaking, they are defined as avoidance of painful feelings and experience of pleasant feelings. Perhaps it would help to bear in mind that while emotions are primitive, raw responses to a given situation, feelings result from processes undergone by emotions in

---

1. Fromm, Erich: *The Art of Loving.*

the psyche. Anyway, when it comes to expressing them (or repressing them) you don't really want to differentiate between them. Since the emotions play a major role in both the negative and positive aspects of our psychic needs, you need to beware that love is not excluded from the list. One might jump to the conclusion that this necessarily involves at least one more person. It does, at some point. But first you may want to go over other emotions that are inherent to human nature. For all practical purposes, it isn't worth making a separation between emotions and feelings. We perfectly realize that, depending on our circumstances, we experience joy, compassion, happiness, elation, despondency, irritability, anger, despair, and so forth. The crucial question is: what do we do about these feelings when they are addressed at ourselves? We obviously should provide a response. You have read above that one manner of dealing with painful feelings consists in avoidance. But avoidance should not be subsumed into denial. You need to acknowledge what you feel and seek the internal cause by questioning yourself until you discover the root, and work on it so that you will not be caught unawares the next time.

Let's see an example of introspection related to one of these feelings:

I feel depressed.

Question 1: What makes me feel depressed?
Answer 1: No matter how hard I try, things never turn
   out the way I want.

Question 2: What exactly do I mean by "'things'"?
Answer 2: Job expectations, my relationship with my
boyfriend . . .

Question 3: Am I failing at both because of the same
reasons?
Answer 3: I don't know.

Question 4: This is about starting to know. What exactly
am I not getting from my job?
Answer 4: Recognition. Sometimes I feel I've made a difference and I don't even get a pat on the shoulder.

Question 5: When this has been the case, have I stood
up for myself?
Answer 5: No.

Question 6: Why not?
Answer 6: I don't know.

Question 7: Let's agree that "I don't know" is not a valid
answer, okay? Maybe I'd rather not know, but I do. So,
again, why not?
Answer 7: Because I don't want to give the impression
that I'm a show-off.

Question 8: Am I a show-off?
Answer 8: No. I just know when I can come up with better ideas than others.

Question 9: What am I afraid may happen if I make my point?

Answer 9: I'm not afraid!

Question 10: There we go again. I'm sure I'm not a show-off. I know when I excel at something, yet I don't speak up. What am I afraid of?

Answer 10: That people will avoid me, thinking that I'm trying to stand out at their expense. I'm afraid of isolation, I guess.

Question 11: Who are "people"?

Answer 11: My co-workers.

Question 12: Not my boss?

Answer 12: No.

Question 13: I said that I don't even get a pat on the shoulder. Would that come from my co-workers?

Answer 13: No, from my boss.

Question 14: Then aren't I mixing two altogether different problems?

Answer 14: Yes.

Question 15: Can I put each problem into perspective?

Answer 15: Yes. I'm afraid that my boss will not take it well if I speak up *and* that my co-workers may avoid me.

Question 16: What do I truthfully think I can do about it?

Answer 16: I could take the risk.

Question 17: What if my fears come true?

Answer 17: It's not really my problem. I don't have to hide my potential or pretend I'm just part of the herd when I'm not actually hurting anybody.

Question 18: What about the particular fear of isolation I mentioned?

Answer 18: I think I can make them see that trying to get legitimate recognition does not entail making them look inefficient.

Question 19: What's not working with my boyfriend?

Answer 19: The sex is great . . .

Question 20: Damn, I'm speaking about what's working. What's *not* working?

Answer 20: He doesn't listen to me.

Question 21: He never listens to me no matter what I'm saying?

Answer 21: He doesn't listen when I'm trying to have a real conversation.

Question 22: What do I mean by a real conversation?

Answer 22: How I feel at work, our plans for the future, starting a family . . .

Question 23: Is all this about me?

Answer 23: In a way, yes.

Question 24: In what way?

Answer 24: For sure, the work part. But our future together concerns both of us.

Question 25: What exactly does he do when I broach our
future together?

Answer 25: He either changes the subject or kisses my
mouth shut and then we end up in bed.

Question 26: Have I ever insisted that I want to discuss
these things?

Answer 26: Not really.

Question 27: Why not, if I feel this is important for me?

Answer 27: Because I'm afraid that if I insist I'll lose him.

Question 28: Like I thought I might "lose" my
co-workers?

Answer 28: It's not the same thing!

Question 29: We'll see about that. What makes me think
that my boyfriend and I have a future together?

Answer 29: We've been living together for three years
now!

Question 30: Has he ever mentioned some kind of future
in these three years?

Answer 30: Well, he does speak of our moving to a more comfortable apartment when we both make more money, and of travelling a little . . .

Question 31: That doesn't seem like the future I have in mind, I know. Why don't I ask him bluntly about his attitude?
Answer 31: Because I feel he may feel pressed and walk out the door.

Question 32: And how would *I* feel if he did that?
Answer 32: Devastated. Alone.

Question 33: Don't I already feel alone when we don't seem to be able to talk?
Answer 33: Yes, deep down I do, but he's there.

Question 34: He's physically there, not there for me. Is it worth putting up with getting no answers to my uncertainties and getting depressed into the bargain?
Answer 34: Probably not.

Question 35: Am I sure the core of the problem with my boyfriend has nothing in common with my problems at work?
Answer 35: Well, the problem seems to be that in both cases I isolate myself for fear of bothering others and thus losing them.

Question 36: So what am I going to do about my
boyfriend?
Answer 36: Straighten things up. If it costs me my relationship, may be it is not the right relationship for me.

There are a number of interesting things about this example. First, the generalization shown by the use of words
such as "things" (Answer 1) and "people" (Answer 10) and
the sentence "He doesn't listen to me" (Answer 20). If you
have read *Living with Stress*, you may remember that Neuro-
Linguistic Programming emphasizes that language should
be as precise as possible, not leaving out such chunks of
reality as may enrich and clarify situations. Second, the
denial that can be read from phrases like "I'm not afraid"
(Answer 9) and "It's not the same thing" (Answer 28). Third,
the attempt at reaching a dead end by uttering an "I don't
know" (Answers 3 and 6). Fourth, the belief that the two
reasons the subject volunteers as probable causes for her
feeling depressed are unrelated (Answers 2 and 28). Fifth,
the effort to give these necessarily painful questions a
positive twist (Answer 19). Last, how deep you need to go
to get to the root of the emotion that is causing the distur-
bance. If you work hard at introspection, you will be able
to respond satisfactorily to your psychic needs, as is clear
from Answers 17 and 35. Use the blank page/s at the end of
this chapter for your exercises in introspection regarding
responsibility to your psychic needs. What makes you feel
happy/joyful? What gives you more satisfaction at work?
List the activities you enjoy the most *after* completing your
introspection exercises.

It may be quite difficult to decide whether or not you **respect** yourself. Fromm reminds us that the origin of the word "respect" is the Latin *respicere* (to look at), and that it consists of the ability to see a person as she is, to be aware of her unique individuality. For the purpose of this discussion, the person in question happens to be you. The trouble with seeing yourself as you are lies in internal distortions fostered by your idealized image (the way you would like to be) and by external peer pressure. In Fromm's admirable words, what may happen is that

> [there is] union [with others] based on conformity with the group, its customs, practices and beliefs. [. . .] The individual self disappears to a large extent [as] the aim is to belong to the herd. Suggestion and propaganda are used in democratic countries to induce conformity. Most people are not even aware [of this]; they believe they are independent. [. . .] The organization (society) prescribes tasks, speed, manner, and feelings [such as] cheerfulness, tolerance, reliability, ambition, and an ability to get along with everybody without friction.[2]

This text was written in 1956. It pains me to say that, if anything, it is truer than ever. If you live in this kind of society, how can you identify your individual differences, let alone express them? Well, it is not a lost cause, though it takes some earnest personal involvement to fight the odds and win.

---

2. Ibid

Let's move from the outside to the inside, from your appearance to your personality. For some reason, only seriously disturbed people—the narcissistic sort—are totally happy with their looks. Not all of them share the tragic fate of Narcissus, the character in Greek myth who lent his name to the maladjustment. The legend goes that Teiresias the seer told Narcissus's mother that the boy would live to a ripe old age provided that he never knew himself. Probably because he was told about the prediction, he took unusual pride in his beauty and refused all the girls and boys who died of love for him. One boy who killed himself on Narcissus's threshold called on the gods for vengeance, and Artemis heard his plea. She led the unmoved lad to a clear spring of water and, as he lay down to rest and quench his thirst, he fell in love with the beautiful boy who stared back at him from the water. He soon realized he was gazing at his own image, as grief gnawed at his heart because that was he but he could not possess himself. Finally, unable to overcome his frustration, he stabbed himself to death, allegedly sighing "Ah youth, beloved in vain, farewell!"

A psychoanalytic approach to narcissism differs from the legend in that two aspects are involved. Supporters of this theory posit that the ego becomes constituted as a psychic unit at the same time as the body schema is constructed. The idea of "unit" in fact also applies to the body, for before this crucial step in our lives, we perceive ourselves as parts—an arm, a leg—yet not as the parts of a whole (our body). Anyway, unity is achieved when the individual has composed a self-image based on an outside model. It could be discussed whether the model replicates the ego, captivates the subject's love from a mirror, or is composed of the primary caregivers' endearing verbal and body language. This is not really important to you. I guess that if you are a narcissist you're not reading this book because you feel you're perfect and need no help. You, who are not a narcissist, should be warned that entering into a relationship with a contemporary male or female Narcissus is a game lost from the start.

Before moving on to what you may feel about your looks, I'd like to say that the right amount of narcissism is indeed healthy. Someone who is totally lacking in narcissism will experience low self-esteem and its concomitant constraints.

All right. You may not be happy about one or more of your bodily features. Typically, women complain of their hair, eye color, breasts, hips, buttocks, and legs. Average men tend to wish they were taller and/or more muscular, while the size and shape of the nose seems to be an issue with both sexes. The bottom line is that we imagine we would look much more attractive if we were different. This may or may not be true. In many cases, features that impress as unattractive or downright ugly if considered in isolation contribute to a harmonious appearance when seen in relation to the whole body. Even so, if a particular feature has given you an inferiority complex or hinders you from leading a normal social life out of a sense of inhibition, you can find a way out.

The body can be sculpted through well-directed gym activity. Hair creams and contact lenses work wonders. Plastic surgery can solve the rest but . . . please consider this solution very carefully before adopting it, and once you have made up your mind, reconsider it once more. Make sure that it is not related to the kind of face or body that society "approves." There's nothing more discouraging for a woman than to pass unnoticed because she has joined the Barbie crew. The same applies to men who get lost in the anonymity of a face and a body that could be interchangeable with anyone else's.

Breast implants, for example, can be removed. Still, ladies, in your pursuit for more fulfilling personal relations, do you really want popularity and attention because of your cup size? On the other hand, with few if any exceptions, face surgeries will stay with you forever. Responsible surgeons (I would venture to say that they are the rule) will not let you choose a "model" in imitation of some famous beauty's features, and will rely on psychological tests to evaluate the consequences of operating on you. However, hateful as you may find your nose, for example, you may discover that a part of your self has gone with your old nose. Therefore, do what you must, but please consider the stakes.

Moreover, there must be parts of your body that you love. Try to give them the place they deserve. A little discreet exhibitionism of your physical assets will enhance your self-confidence in ways you cannot even dream of. Beauty enters through the eyes. This saying should not be understood literally. No one falls for a marble Venus or Apollo. It just points to the fact that a pleasant appearance and an engaging, lively attitude will give you better chances of approaching others. The chances that an initial approach may develop into a relationship are conditioned by what you carry *inside.*

This brings us to your personality. If you abide by group conformity (perhaps it would help to reread Fromm's words on p. 12), you have renounced your uniqueness and, consequently, have nothing to offer that others have not. Hard as this may sound, you are expendable. Any other member of the herd can replace you with no one noticing the difference, because there is no difference. You need to fight tooth and nail to avoid drifting with the tide. Besides being **you**, be clear about what you are like. As is the case with your body, your personality/character may not make you totally happy. You need to gain awareness of positive and negative aspects, and work on the latter. Nobody is perfect, yet everything is perfectible. Personality and character are not exactly the same. You may find ample information about personality in *Living with Stress,* the first book in this series. To avoid repetition, I will only say here that, among the many theories about personality development, I find consistency in the one that posits that personality results from the interaction between inherited traits and the social environment in which we live. In my view, character is an aspect of personality. As a system of personal traits, it develops over time, does not change quickly—though it can change, whereas personality cannot—and is shown through observable behavior. For practical purposes, let's consider them together and see what you identify with.

Here is a list of personality/character traits. Tick the ones you think apply to you, and decide whether you deem them positive or negative. Remember this book belongs to you and need not be shared with anyone else, so don't let your idealized image trick you into choosing traits that you would like to have. If you can think of others out of the list, do not hesitate to add them.

You view yourself as

- ☐ Concrete
- ☐ Ambitious
- ☐ Outspoken
- ☐ Affectionate
- ☐ Friendly
- ☐ Responsible
- ☐ Tormented
- ☐ Conservative
- ☐ Relaxed
- ☐ Logical
- ☐ Active
- ☐ Cold
- ☐ Lively
- ☐ Humorous
- ☐ Empathetic
- ☐ Emotional
- ☐ Jealous
- ☐ Envious
- ☐ Romantic
- ☐ Playful
- ☐ Assertive
- ☐ Independent
- ☐ Collaborative
- ☐ Cautious
- ☐ Adventurous
- ☐ Moody

- ☐ Predictable
- ☐ Introspective
- ☐ Reliable
- ☐ Distrustful
- ☐ Earnest
- ☐ Skeptical
- ☐ Optimistic
- ☐ Pessimistic
- ☐ Tidy
- ☐ Factual
- ☐ Disorganized
- ☐ Speculative
- ☐ Impulsive
- ☐ Indecisive
- ☐ Analytic
- ☐ Rational
- ☐ Anxious
- ☐ Cheerful
- ☐ Easy-going
- ☐ Irrational
- ☐ Distracted
- ☐ Productive
- ☐ Stubborn
- ☐ Overachieving
- ☐ Underachieving
- ☐ Spontaneous
- ☐ Patient
- ☐ Sensible
- ☐ Sensitive
- ☐ Hard-working

☐ Oversensitive
☐ Reserved
☐ Flexible
☐ Generous

You now need to consider that most personality/character traits are neither positive nor negative in themselves, but that their classification depends on the context in which they appear. For example, "stubborn" proves negative when you won't listen to reason, but may turn positive if your stubbornness prevents you from being talked into doing things you think wrong, harmful, immoral, or dangerous. By the same token, it may sound great to be "patient" unless your patience leads you to put up with abuse of some kind or other.

Assuming that you have reached the point when you see yourself as you really are, let's try to find out whether you respect yourself according to a definition that differs from Fromm's: *feel or show regard for*. If you take care of yourself in the ways discussed earlier on *and* accept your uniqueness, we may agree that self-respect has been accomplished.

The last basic constituent of love is **knowledge**. "I have to know [...] myself objectively in order to be able to see [my] reality, or rather, to overcome the illusions, the irrationally distorted picture I have [of myself]."[3]

"Objectively" is the key word. It means that you need to stand outside yourself, in a manner of speaking, and renounce your subjectivity while you watch what is, for

---

3. Ibid

this purpose, an object. The illusions and the distorted picture may stem from either your idealized image (an overly positive view) or from a lack in the necessary amount of narcissism, in which case you would rate the "object" (you) as valueless.

Everything that you have read and practiced so far will help you to know yourself objectively. A correct reading of your conclusions will ensure that you have done what is necessary to hold a harmonious relationship with yourself. You are now ready to look into your relationships with others.

I TAKE CARE OF MY SOUL BY ...

I TAKE CARE OF MY BODY BY ...

AN INTROSPECTIVE EXERCISE INTO MY PSYCHIC NEEDS

THE ACTIVITIES I ENJOY THE MOST

2

Parents and Children

Mother you had me but I never had you
—John Lennon

In the previous chapter I mentioned that it takes a while before we begin to perceive ourselves as a unit. When we are babies ruled by primitive instincts alone we don't identify people but experience pleasure and displeasure as sensations—raw, unprocessed feelings, remember? Therefore, a mother figure stands for everything that provides us with satisfaction and security. What we will later identify as "mother" is, for a period of our lives, food, warmth, and a pleasant sensation of comfort.

According to Fromm,

The outside reality, persons, or things have meaning only in terms of their satisfying or frustrating the inner state of the body. Real is only what is within; what is outside is real only in terms of my needs—never in terms of its own qualities or needs.[4]

At this stage of development, the child feels that the father is some kind of useful "means of transport" that can bring her near objects that attract her attention. A clever pediatrician described the father as a comfortable, safe moving ladder.

Physical contact, loving words, praise, patience and, above all, emotional balance will lay the best possible foundations for rewarding relationships between parents and children. Still, as our manners of relating to others (and children *are* others, not extensions of their parents) are heavily rooted in our childhood relationships with our parents, we may find ourselves at a disadvantage if our early memories or unconscious inscriptions are at odds with good parenting. If this were the case, perhaps it would be best to heal our wounds by looking back and reinterpreting the past to understand what went wrong before bringing a child into the world. Unless we internally solve pending issues with our own parents, we tend to make one of two mistakes that will undermine our children's independent perceptions in adolescence and adulthood. Namely, we consciously or unconsciously do either exactly the same as or exactly the opposite to our parents' choices. No wonder Freud advocated the inclusion of three generations to figure out why an individual was afflicted with certain anxieties.

---

4. Ibid

I have perhaps harped on the concept of responsibility to the limit of endurance, yet I need to stretch the point one inch further and ask you to consider that, besides all the meanings explored so far, responsibility is also the addition of response + ability: the ability to respond.

In practice, this ability is transmitted to the child through parental behavior rather than through lectures about behavior. The contradiction implicit in "Do as I say, not as I do" throws the child into confusion and ambivalence that will later deteriorate the whole range of her relationships.

In Charles Dickens's *David Copperfield*, the protagonist's widowed mother remarries when her only son David has not yet turned seven. Although she loves him dearly, she allows her new husband to discipline David in accordance to the gentleman's notions about good parenting, best described as "spare the rod and spoil the child." Accordingly, Mr. Murdstone, who proffered to have the child's best interest in mind, flogged him, inflicted psychological torture on him, and finally sent him away to boarding school, with David's mother watching on, no doubt loving him, yet doing nothing to protect him.

This is how David felt when he returned home after his mother's wedding and honeymoon, for he had been conveniently put out of the way.

God help me, I might have been improved for my whole life, I might have been made another creature perhaps, for life, by a kind word at that season. A word of encouragement and explanation, of pity for my childish ignorance, of welcome home, of reassurance to me that it was home, might have made me dutiful to him in my heart henceforth, instead of in my hypocritical outside, and might have made me respect instead of hate him. I thought my mother was sorry to see me standing in the room so scared and strange, and that, presently, when I stole to a chair, she followed me with her eyes more sorrowfully still—missing, perhaps, some freedom in my childish tread—but the word was not spoken, and the time for it was gone.

Dickens's literary children and parents offer an impressive sampler of incomprehension and unhappiness, but this particular passage goes to show that a child's future may be seriously compromised by parental behavior in her childhood. We would all agree that probably parents and stepparents know better in the 21st century. However, even if the forms are different, the essence remains pretty much the same in many family structures.

Interestingly, Fromm posits that while the mother's love is unconditional, the father's has to be earned. He says that "to be loved because one deserves it always leaves doubt, a bitter feeling that one is not loved for oneself, but only because one pleases."

If this is true, the child may be burdened for life with the belief that she must please at any cost whenever she wants to preserve a relationship. This might lead to blind obedience and submission in situations in which the internalized father figure raises its head as a reminder that one risks abandonment if one does not comply. The fictive threat of the withdrawal of fatherly love transferred to other relationships will stifle individuality and subjectivity. In other words, you will sacrifice your uniqueness in the hope that a given relationship will thrive.

Fromm also offers two thought-provoking statements about a mother's role:

> Part of the mother's love should be the wish that the child become independent and eventually separate from her. Father's love should be patient and tolerant rather than threatening and authoritarian.[5]

Let us start at the end. In a way, this remark about fatherly love seems to contradict the fact that his love has to be earned through blindly fulfilling his expectations. In any case, it sounds much more reassuring and positive than the previous assertion. In regard to the mother's love, he also points out that "a selfish mother is overconcerned not because she loves the child too much but because she has to compensate for her lack of capacity to love him at all."[6]

This goes to prove my belief that a mother's love for her child is not mechanically born together with the baby. If I were to carry this notion a little further, it would confirm some medical observations about mothers who live in constant dread of their children catching mortal diseases or having terrible accidents. Experts explain such exaggerated fears as unconscious desires to somehow "kill" the child. It goes without saying that here we are looking at

5. Ibid
6. Ibid

pathological reactions that sons and daughters should ignore for the sake of their own peace of mind.

Going back to the issue of independence and separation, I'm afraid that some developed societies encourage their young to sever practically all bonds from their family of origin. Custom has established that it is desirable for teenagers to go away to college in another city or state. While this may be an advantage from the point of view of their education and subsequent career goals, it estranges them from their parents as they seldom come home owing to distance, study commitments, part-time jobs that help pay for tuition, and involvement in a new, exciting environment free of curfew and grounding. Other reasons may be the lure of partying and peer group pressure (When in Rome, do as the Romans do).

If children and parents get together for Christmas and/or New Year—that is, once a year—the extended family hardly stands a chance of reunion. Most probably brothers, sisters, uncles, aunts, and cousins have long parted ways.

Even before this kind of separation takes place, at some point, while teenagers are still living at the family home, physical contact is restricted to very special occasions. Either the parents refrain from lavishly hugging and kissing their sons and daughters as they used to do when they were young kids or the teenagers themselves shun contact *because* now that they have grown older they feel it's awkward. There comes the time when the relationship rests on not very frequent phone calls and an occasional greeting card or e-mail.

In other words, this family model serves as a launching

platform for "rockets" whose destiny no one can predict, and disintegrates once this purpose has been achieved. If the need arises for a forced return (a parent's severe illness requiring care, a son's or daughter's difficult divorce or dire economic straits), the relationship will probably be strained. It may or may not regain the trust and intimacy of former days. There is the risk that no one will feel happy, because by now parents and children look upon one another as complete strangers.

You may feel that this is normal. If by "normal" you mean "standard" or "the norm" (the way everyone lives in your society), you're right. However, this model breeds poor communication, shallow emotional commitment, reluctance to share your worries with those who should be your natural source of comfort and advice, and a deeply buried feeling of loneliness. All of this is in total contradiction with care, responsibility, respect, and knowledge, the notions that were developed in Chapter 1 to clarify your relationship with yourself. Here you need to substitute parents/child/children for "you"/"yourself".

I am not suggesting that you tie your children to your apron strings or cripple their growth and freedom. But perhaps you would like to reconsider your relationship with your parents/children. Answer the questionnaire on the pages at the end of the chapter to have a clearer idea of the kind of family relationships you have built/are building.

In short, your relationship with your parents or children could be greatly improved if you reviewed the matrix of your own family. Mainstream does not necessarily mean "the only acceptable way to go about things."

One issue that calls for thoughtful consideration is that of roles. We seem to have evolved from a family structure with clearly defined roles (father = breadwinner/mother = caregiver) into another in which all roles, including the children's, are interchangeable. Flexibility is indeed necessary in a world with so many one-parent families, blended families, stay-at-home fathers, same-sex parents, and breadwinning mothers. Still, unless there is some method within the role flexibility, children tend to lose sight of behavioral models and patterns. Rather, they learn that anything goes, or that the various people composing the family are pretty much the same. By extension, they may apply this notion to their future relationships and fail where they expected to succeed. It will take time for them to find out what went awry, and they may even never know as they bounce from one frustrated relationship to another.

Let's take a look at a different kind of family, one in which abuse is the keyword. Some people believe that abuse is only physical (blows and/or sexual abuse). In the developed societies mentioned above, paranoid fears that a parent is improperly touching his/her child lead one to believe that this type of perversion must be fairly common. Unfortunately, dread of being accused of improper conduct must also contribute to parents' refraining from showing their love through cuddling and kisses.

On the other hand, psychological abuse, when it is not glaring, tends to pass unnoticed. Many families in which, for example, members scream invectives at each other, violate privacy, constantly break promises, and endanger economic stability by squandering their earnings would be shocked to hear that all this is yet another form of abuse.

A victim of physical abuse can recognize what is going on and resort to the proper channels of protection. If only it were true that the solution is that simple! To begin with, when the victim is a very young child, the abusive parent, elder sibling, or relative will usually seduce her before abusing her, so her moral standards, still in the making, will not help her realize that she's being subjected to perverse practices. Moreover, ambivalent love-hate feelings for her abuser may make her put up with what she perhaps senses is "weird" because she does not want to lose the abuser's "love." And sometimes, if the victim plucks up courage to complain to a parent (typically the mother), she may face violent rebuke and rejection. Most women will not believe that a family member has a perverse psychic structure. Moreover, abusers' wives tend to turn a blind eye on what they know is true because confronting reality will entail losing their husband, something they cannot bear. No doubt the problem becomes more complex when the abusive husband is not the victim's father.

I am describing a very sick relationship that involves the whole family. It has been repeatedly said that abusers cannot be cured, so if you are one, I can only appeal to your sense of decency and ask you to avoid situations in which you might be free to indulge in your disease. If you are a witness, or the victim—your child, sister, or brother—has come to you for help, you need to stop the abuse by doing what it takes. Otherwise, you yourself are an abuser by proxy.

Perhaps you are now an adult, an ex-victim who man-aged to erase/repress memories of childhood abuse and move on. In your unconscious mind, these memories will shape your present and future relationships. You will become wary of whoever approaches you and suspect that you may get badly hurt again. Or else you will entice new friends and acquaintances through equivocal attitudes that may lead them on, with you screaming blue murder because "that's not what you meant." The long and the short of it is that you have slim chances of engaging in fulfilling relationships unless a) you confront your abuser no matter how much time has passed and, b) you seek counseling to work out the hatred, fear, and guilt you're carrying inside you. Of course you're not guilty of what happened to you. Still, many victims, in their effort to protect their idealized image of the abuser prefer to think it was their own fault, not to speak of those who were bluntly accused of having brought it upon themselves.

Regarding psychological abuse, the family has the chance to talk about it. Honest discussion of what bothers you can mend many of these situations provided that everyone concerned is really committed to improving frayed relationships. However, just as it is believed that most physical abusers were abused as children, it is also thought that psychological abusers suffered some kind of repeated humiliation in their childhood. Thus they came to regard their behavior as normal, the difference with the other case being that, unless there is a mental condition, they can see reason in the course of as many verbal exchanges as are necessary. In sum, resignation is definitely the worst choice. Abuse within the family weighs heavily on all other relationships.

QUESTIONNAIRE FOR PARENTS

1. When your young child/children have/had trouble with their school assignments, you
   a) made it clear that they had to manage on their own.
   b) helped them understand what was required of them and encouraged them to do the assignments once they felt confident they knew how to handle them.
   c) felt sorry at their anguish and did the assignments for them.

2. You think/thought that
   a) it's never too early to make a child feel independent.
   b) independence may be a double-edged weapon if the child is/was too young to have full comprehension of potential dangers.
   c) independence is gradually taught and acquired, so even a very young child can be given responsibility for easy, safe tasks at home.

3. Do/did you agree that
   a) children should be praised when they do/did things right?
   b) it's not necessary to praise children when they do things right because that's simply what is/was expected of them?
   c) praise spoils children, considering that they won't get it often when they leave home?

4. Young children should
   a) be exposed to real life problems and dangers as early as possible or else they won't know how to deal with them later on.
   b) be warned of real life problems and dangers and have the chance of discussing them with you, but you shouldn't create situations that might expose them to such problems.
   c) remain ignorant of real life problems until they can understand their full implications.

5. Young children and teenagers should
   a) not make any choices unless you approve of them.
   b) choose freely regardless of what's at stake, and put up with the consequences if they have made the wrong choice.
   c) choose freely depending on what's at stake, but discuss the options with you first.

6. You are raising/raised your children
   a) constantly reminding them that eventually they will have to stand on their own feet, so they'd better start to do so as early as possible.
   b) encouraging them to live independent lives, but letting them know that you will/would always be there for them.
   c) teaching them that independence goes hand in hand with responsibility, so they need to think whether they are ready to take responsibility for their independent decisions.

7. If your college-age children are still living at home, do you
   a) resent it because you feel they interfere with your life?
   b) let them know that they will have to abide by your rules, since their lifestyle is different now and you will not put up with loud music at any hour, friends coming in and out or sleeping over without warning, etc?
   c) make them feel that they are overstaying their welcome?

8. When your children have grown up and left home, do you
   a) make sure they feel you are still a family and tell them that the type of relationship may have changed but that your love for them has not?
   b) feel quite happy that you don't see them or talk to them often, because in a way you think your parental role is over once they're on their own?
   c) expect some kind of detailed report of their movements and feel hurt/offended if you don't get it?

9. Do you indicate to your grown-up children that
   a) you expect moral support/financial help in return for having given them the best years of your life?
   b) families should keep close enough not to lose the emotional bonds that constituted the family in the first place?
   c) you feel lonely/lost/helpless?

10. If you are divorced,
    a) have you explained to your children (young or grown-up) what led to the break-up in the most objective way possible?
    b) have you only broken the news to them without explanations because you feel it's a private matter between you and your spouse?
    c) have you blamed it on your spouse, even if it was really mostly his/her decision?

There are no right or wrong answers to the above questions. However, you will find comments on the answers at the end of this chapter. Perhaps you would like to reconsider the implications of your answers after reading the comments.

QUESTIONNAIRE FOR GROWN-UP SONS/DAUGHTERS

1. When you think of your childhood, what do you remember more clearly?
   a) how happy you were.
   b) Your parents/One parent insisting that you do things you hated.
   c) Nothing in particular.

2. As a child, what time of the week did you enjoy the most?
   a) Weekdays, because you spent them at school with your friends.
   b) Weekends, because you enjoyed leisure time with your family, particularly your parents.
   c) Special weekdays because you had sports or other activities that kept you away from home for longer hours than usual.

3. When you were a young child, your parents/one parent
   a) put you to bed and read you or told you a bedtime story.
   b) put you to bed and turned off the light in your room.
   c) sent you to bed on your own.

4. How did you choose your childhood friends?
    a) On the basis of empathy/similar likes and dislikes.
    b) Your parents chose them for you.
    c) You didn't have friends, just schoolmates.

5. As a teenager, your parents
    a) kept you on a short leash.
    b) did not demand that you tell them where and with whom you hung out.
    c) explained to you the dangers of certain company and places.

6. When you grew up,
    a) you grabbed the first opportunity to move out from home.
    b) you moved out from home, but missed your parents until you got used to your new surroundings, and let your parents know how you felt.
    c) you stayed at home and expected your parents/ parent to take care of your meals, washing, etc. You mostly used your home as a rent-free motel.

7. When you left home, you
    a) often visited.
    b) phoned from time to time.
    c) tended to put off your parents visiting you if they offered to come.

8. As a grown-up, perhaps with a family of your own, you
   a) would not hesitate to assist your parents/parent should they need financial help or personal care.
   b) feel you can't divert time or money to your parents/parent.
   c) could assist them, but you feel you have too little in common with them at this time of your life, so you don't really owe them anything.

9. You
   a) often talk about your parents (dead or alive)
   b) prefer not to talk about your parents.
   c) tend to "improve" on your parents' real character and circumstances if you must talk about them.

10. You
   a) feel rather uncomfortable if your parents kiss you heartily.
   b) understand that elderly people need loving physical contact as children do.
   c) think a strict, old-school, no-nonsense upbringing works just fine.

There are no right or wrong answers to the above questions. However, you will find comments on the answers at the end of this chapter. Perhaps you would like to reconsider the implications of your answers after reading the comments.

COMMENTS ON THE QUESTIONNAIRE FOR PARENTS

1.a. This answer establishes an abrupt divide between parents and children. If this is your view, you're implicitly telling your children that they have a separate life in which you wish no part. The idea that they should manage on their own will extend, in their mind, to other aspects of their life, so they will not come to you if they're bullied at school or if they are asked by friends to lie for them, for example. Naturally, if your children bring bad grades, you will feel exceedingly angry, not to speak of what you'll say if they come home with a black eye or get into trouble for mischievous behavior. This attitude on your part implies that you regard the child as an adult, and he is definitely not that. Moreover, your anger/disappointment at the child's grades or wrong choices will throw her into confusion, since you first told her to manage alone and now you reproach her because of the way she managed. It's okay to encourage independence, but it's certainly not advisable to offer no guidance.

1.b. If you have chosen this answer, your message to your child is that she needs to do what is asked of her, as you have already finished school and have no intention to restart. However, you're also telling her that she can turn to you for advice when at a loss, and that you are happy to help so that she can do what she must. Again, the idea that she is free to ask will extend to all areas of life, so when confronted with life problems that go beyond her comprehension or capacity of decision, the child will come to you. This will save you both much unpleasantness in the long run, with the added benefit that you and your child will establish a mutual bond of trust. When established at an early age, this bond tends to last for life and, at some point, your adult son/daughter will gladly "parent" you.

1.c. This amounts to becoming a "crutch" on which your child can comfortably lean whenever she feels insecure. In all likelihood, this will turn out to be the case all the time. Consider that patients who have undergone a hip replacement, for example, are encouraged to walk without artificial aids as soon as possible, for fear that they think of their crutch as their real leg. In addition, letting your child know that she deserves pity is humiliating, as what you're conveying is that the child is somehow handicapped. If your attitude to homework develops into a more general behavior, your child may never do anything by herself. She will become completely dependent on you, and I don't think you want that. You may delude yourself into believing that things will change when the child grows up. Well, they won't, because you have established a pattern in her psyche. When you're no longer there to do things for her, she'll grab at the first person that can take your place by marrying a surrogate parent, for instance.

2.a. It all depends on what you mean by "independent." To be truly independent, an individual needs to fully understand the problem (the life situation she is confronting) and the consequences of her decision. By definition, infants are incapable of abstract thought—and so are many adults, but this is not what we are discussing—and need teaching and guidance. When you're sure that they have learned to the extent an infant can; that is, not through the intellect but through the senses, it's safe to encourage their independence within the restricted field of their experience.

2.b. This is true, so rather safe than sorry. However, if you live in constant fear that your child will come to harm because of potential dangers, you may be thwarting her natural curiosity and concomitant trial-and-error learning. Thus as long as you make sure that there is no serious danger, you may encourage your child's self-confidence by letting her try to do some things by herself, with you watching discreetly. Then she will improve her amount of tolerance to frustration when she doesn't succeed, and will not grow into an all-fearing individual. Remember that your children shape their feelings on yours. You want to instill caution, not fear.

2.c. I dare say this is the best way to raise a responsible, independent child. At the same time, it demands a lot of effort and planning on your part, as you need to carefully weigh the pros and cons of every task you entrust her. Still, parenting, like teaching, is about the adult going out of her way for a considerable period of time so that she can later on stand aside and trust that the child will do things right with minimum supervision. If you feel that you don't have that much time to spend, think of the time you will have to spend in years to come, besides fretting at the risks the child might inadvertently face. It's up to you to do the math.

3.a. If children are praised for doing things right, they will learn the difference between success and failure. Besides, children love praise, because they love to please. Well-earned praise will encourage them to do things right at all times, though of course outcomes will vary depending on the circumstances. Still, praise makes children feel self-confident and proud of their own ability to do certain things, so when they fail they will willingly try again if properly guided. Mind, though, that meaningless praise (praise offered just for the sake of it) voids its essence to the point that it is not recorded as such.

3.b. If you assume this, your child may feel discouraged, wondering what's the use of making her best effort if nobody notices it. As adults, we know that the reward of work well done is satisfaction in the results. However, this is something that we learn gradually and that involves a positive, realistic position before life. A young child needs to learn that we feel good when we do things right and frustrated/unhappy when we don't. At an early age, this feeling is prompted by praise and positive criticism respectively. Then if you simply don't react to the outcome of the child's actions, she will feel a) that you don't care one way or the other and, b) that you don't love her, since very young children tend to do things because they want to please their parents. Their motivation is love. On the other hand, if you rebuke the child when she does things wrong but don't praise her when she does them right, she will try to succeed just to avoid your lectures/punishment. This behavior may become deeply ingrained and affect all her future relationships.

3.c. You really cannot anticipate whether or not your child will earn praise in the future. Perhaps out of your own experience you're trying to spare her future disappointment by reproducing at home your notion of the "world." Still, particularly because the "world" may be so hard on us, home should be a haven. While it is true that it is your parental duty to prepare your child for the ugliness/meanness she will come across in life, it is no less true that you are establishing the basis of her relationship with you. What you see as a useful lesson about reality may be perceived as indifference, and repaid in the same way.

4.a. The trouble is that there is no inscription of "danger" and "problem" in very young children. If you expose them to things they do not understand for what they really are, the chances are that children may be physically or psychically hurt. On the other hand, as the child does have a life, she will be exposed to dangers and problems inside the scope of her daily experiences, so there's probably no need to expand these boundaries. They will expand by themselves as the child grows up. Unprotective parents seem to have the same effects as do overprotective parents. Exposure without explanations, teaching, guidance, and supervision in no way ensures that the child will be able to cope with anything. At some point, your son/daughter may well blame you for having been traumatized through exposure to life situations he/she was unable to handle.

4.b. This shows good comprehension of the early childhood stage. If this is your choice, your children will acquire self-confidence and trust your judgement and advice, for they will never feel abandoned or neglected. Nothing is more terrifying to a child than the idea that she's not safe with her parents around. Since you're building basic behavior patterns that will in all likelihood shape your child's notions about parenting, you will be exercising a positive influence on two generations.

4.c. You may find it difficult to turn your child into a would-be Snow White in her crystal box. While you may lock your door against the evils of this world, they will slip in through the window. Much as you control exposure, television and the Internet put your child in contact with all sorts of situations. Your child will naturally turn to you in an attempt to understand what's going on. If you refuse to answer her questions, she will build hypotheses of her own, probably with the help of other children in the same situation. Such hypotheses are often more terrifying than the truth, as shown in Dan De Lillo's *Falling Man*. And even if you succeeded in preserving your child from reality, you would be denying her the tools and awareness she will need to live an acceptable life. Surely you can always offer an explanation suited to her age. Again, in the absence of reasons, the future adult may fill comprehension gaps with imaginary answers, something that she will apply to her manners of relating to others.

5.a. Not all choices have the same implications. Surely a child/teenager can make independent choices within a certain range of issues and feel that it's all right if she makes a mistake, for we learn from our mistakes. If you restrict your child's freedom to this extent, you a) are making it clear to her that you have no confidence whatsoever in her good judgement; b) are suggesting that you have no confidence in what *you* taught her, since her choices will supposedly be based on your principles and, c) will appear as a tyrannical parent, one who says, "It's either my way or no way at all." Giving your child the freedom to make mistakes is important, and it's good for her to get trained in recognizing them as such and mending them. Otherwise, the first mistake may be really serious and even unmanageable.

5.b. This answer puts parenting in abeyance. Your children/teens may feel elated at the possibility of free choice while not being totally aware of the meaning of "putting up with the consequences." When you do this, your message is "I'm done with my parental job, so don't bother me with questions and don't come crying to me if things go wrong." The trouble is that if things do go wrong (and at some point they will if this is your policy), you will feel exceedingly angry/ embarrassed/disappointed and will definitely want to do something about it. Parents' contradictory attitudes make children feel that dad/mom are not dependable. At best, children will find other, more reliable adults to turn to. At worst, they may feel that no one can be trusted. Lack of trust kills a relationship from the very start.

5.c. Children and teenagers appreciate the opportunity of being listened to, particularly when they need to make a decision. If given the chance to discuss the options with their parents, they feel respected and show respect in return. Even if their final choice differs from their parents', they know that they will be supported and understood. They also know that the wrong decision will not bring on retribution but a new discussion to evaluate the situation anew. It's also good for children and teenagers to know that some decisions are non-negotiable because they still lack the necessary experience.

6.a. One attractive thing about childhood is that we live in two worlds at once: the real world, and that of our imagination and fantasy. A normal child is perfectly able to tell the difference between both. It would be a pity to spoil his enjoyment of "as if" by constantly reminding him of responsibilities that are not yet hers. Remember the saying "All work and no play makes Jack a dull boy"? A dull child may grow into an embittered adult whose company people will most probably shun.

6.b. This notion fills children with confidence, but perhaps you're making a promise that you may not be able to keep. "Always" is a big word. Sometimes life gets in the way of good intentions. It's certainly advisable to encourage independence in children while letting them know that they can count on you, but perhaps it's wise to leave "always" and "never" out of the picture. Children cling to the literal meaning of words, and when promises made to them are broken, even for the best of reasons, they tend to feel betrayed. This makes them suspicious of promises in general, or else makes them feel that they can promise lightly, as it's okay to go back on promises. Either behavior will be reflected in their relationship with you and with others.

6.c. You have read practically everything that can be said about responsibility. Reminding your child about the connection between independence and responsibility will help her weigh her decisions carefully and diminish the odds of her making irreparable mistakes. As an additional bonus, you will feel that you fulfilled your parental role without underestimating or ignoring your child's intelligence and judgement.

7.a. Your children are now young men/women whose lifestyle probably differs from yours (and there is cause to worry if it doesn't!). However, there may be good reasons for their living at home while they attend college. Resenting their presence without discussing the reasons won't lead you anywhere. You may find that they are being sensible, in which case you can live together in harmony if you establish a number of simple rules about the things that bother you. Once more, if you feel that your sons/daughters interfere with your life, you have unconsciously decided that you can "retire" from your "job" as a parent. Think that this may encourage them to consider "retiring" from their filial role.

7.b. Letting your grown-up children know that they're living at *your* home not at some motel reinforces the idea that, ultimately, they are welcome to stay as long as they don't appropriate the place. This is a way of establishing a clear divide between the elderly and the young. Though you can now exchange opinions and enjoy discussions with your children on an equal standing, that does not mean that they don't owe you respect both as parents and owners of the house/apartment. If they had chosen to live with someone else, the same degree of respect would be demanded. In other words, that you are parents should not put you at a disadvantage.

7.c. Parents who opt for this choice prefer dropping verbal or behavioral hints to having a straightforward, mature conversation with their children. They may sing the praises of a young relative "who is living away from home and do-ing great in college," "forget" to set the extra place at the table, "inadvertently" clutter their son's/daughter's room with discarded furniture, for example, and so forth. If asked by the child whether they feel uncomfortable with the situation, these parents will probably deny it and even feel slighted at the remark. The double message confuses the child for a short time only. She soon realizes that she's no longer wanted, and will surely make the necessary ar-rangements to leave in no time. No doubt the parents will feel delighted to have achieved their goal without having had to spell it out, but the psychic damage done to the child may stay with her forever, tainting her other relationships with distrust.

8.a. This strengthens the notion of family that you have probably been building all along. When sons and daughters have the certainty that their bonds with their parents are bulletproof independently of physical proximity, they are prepared to face the world with very good chances of success. In due time, they are also ready to start a family without qualms, for they will rely on the internalized safety net provided by you.

8.b. Again, this is the "retirement" effect. That your children are now living their lives as independent adults does not mean burning bridges. In a way, you're washing your hands of them, so don't complain if they wash theirs of you. What goes around comes around, as the saying goes.

8.c. Perhaps you haven't come to terms with the fact that your children have grown up. A balance is needed between what they wish to share and what they'd rather keep to themselves. Hovering over your children all the time will estrange them from you, so insistence and demands on your part will make you suffer more than you are suffering already. Learning to cope with this new stage of your life ("the empty nest") may be hard, but there's no turning back the clock. It should indeed worry you if your children could not take a step without telling you about it. This would mean that you failed to raise a responsible, independent human being.

9.a. If you do so, you are trying to collect a debt that I call "unpayable." Open parental claims of this sort typically encourage answers like "I did not ask to be born." If your parenting has been based on love according to the definition made in Chapter 1, your children will spontaneously come to you in your time of need. The so-called "ungrateful children" are the product of parents' mistakes. We have already agreed that nobody is perfect. Still, if you feel you need to indicate to your children that they "owe" you, you probably feel unsure that you have offered your unconditional love.

9.b. In their enthusiasm to begin a new, important part of their lives, youngsters tend to take family bonds for granted. They know that mom and dad (together or separately) will always be there for them. "There" may well appear in their fantasy as a closet with the parents neatly placed on hangers, waiting for the children to come and "wear" them. There's no harm in reminding them that family bonds need communication and proximity to keep strong.

9.c. Your grown-up children may feel desperately helpless themselves if you indicate this to them. Such cries for help are in fact addressed to "parents"; that is, to protective figures. Your children are in no position to protect anybody but themselves—hopefully—until they become full-blown adults or parents. You need to look into your own processes of maturity and find out what makes you so weak at this precise moment. Sometimes this attitude works as a sort of "moral blackmail" intending to fill children with guilt for having "abandoned" the parent. If you believe this underlies your remarks about loneliness, etc. perhaps you should review the role each member of the family played before your child left. You may find that the roles were inverted, and that your child was in some way parenting you. It's not too late to put things back in place.

10.a. An affirmative answer to this question means that your children were not a battleground when the divorce came through, and that you were perfectly aware that splitting with your ex did not entail forcing a split between him/her and the children.

10.b. When children aren't given an explanation about the causes of their parents' divorce, they often think that they are to blame. Because the mind accepts no logical gaps, something called "magic thought" fills in the blanks with plausible yet mistakenly linked episodes. Thus, a child may believe that her parents have divorced because she misbehaved. All children misbehave, so the episode in question is true but not the linking "because." An alternative to this self-concocted explanation is laying the blame on a character trait of either parent, particularly if the other parent has often criticized this. In both cases the child's anxiety rises to alarming levels, especially if she bottles up her feelings about the divorce.

10.c. It may be difficult to resist blackening the character of a now hated spouse in the hope that you may deprive him/her of your children's love. Unless there were issues with the children too, you need to accept that a spouse and a parent play different roles and that while a spouse can be dispensed with and eventually replaced, a parent cannot.

You may succeed in estranging your children from your ex for some time, but at some point you yourself may become the butt of their hatred for doing so.

COMMENTS ON THE QUESTIONNAIRE FOR GROWN-UP SONS/DAUGHTERS

1.a. Happy childhood memories may help you cope with present difficulties. Revisiting these memories and taking momentary refuge in them will strengthen your resolution to deal with problems. You know from experience that happiness can be achieved, so you will probably struggle against adversity with great conviction. On the other hand, if you feel nostalgic about your past as a child, you may have to put things in perspective. The idea is not yearning for a "lost" time of your life, but to treasure it as a source of hope about the possibility of regaining happiness in your adult life.

1.b. If you remember your parents too often, perhaps you feel that you are still a "child." You may need to work on your self-confidence and ability to confront situations standing on your own two feet, for it is maturity rather than age that proves you have succeeded in reaching adulthood. Still, if your memories keep going back to what you think were negative aspects of your parents (their wanting to force your will, for example), you may need to revisit the concrete instances of this behavior. Your parents may have insisted on your doing things that you had to learn for your own good, even if you found them hateful at the time. Make a list of what was involved. Which of these things aided your healthy transition from childhood into adolescence and from adolescence into adulthood? Which were useless parental whims that led to nothing? Even the latter can be put to good use: don't do the same to your children.

1.c. This may mean that you have locked the "childhood compartment" in your memory and thrown away the key. Far from indicating that you had an ordinary childhood, this obliteration of memories may point to painful moments that you fear will arouse the same past anxiety if you relive them in your mind. Blocking memories is a short-effect avoidance technique. The formations of the unconscious (dreams, slips of the tongue, forgetting other seemingly unrelated things, etc.) and your present attitude to life issues thrust hard to remind you of such moments. Perhaps you need to make a conscious effort to bring your childhood to the focus of the mind and work out what really happened, with the help of your parents, siblings, other trusted relatives, or professional counseling.

2.a. You seem to have found life at school more fulfilling than life at home, and better containment from your friends/ teachers than from your family. In some way, you may have turned school into "home." Hundreds of reasons may account for this, such as having had little attention from busy parents, frequent fights between them, etc. Whatever the reasons, preferring an environment outside home may have stuck with you. See whether you still spend as much time as possible away from home. Think that if you're married/

have children living with you, you may be pushing them in the same direction, a vicious circle that considerably weakens family relationships.

2.b. You probably had a happy childhood and a great relationship with your parents. Those past weekends probably drive you to make the most of your present weekends, when the kind of fun may be different, but is still fun. In addition, you're probably immune to the "Sunday blues". Your experience enhances your social life and, if you have children (or when you have them), you will establish the same pattern of relationships with them.

2.c. It seems clear that you didn't have a great time at home. However, the fact that you devoted your time to positive activities rather than hanging out on the streets without purpose shows that your parents probably gave you the tools to make the right choices. Perhaps you don't think the world of them, but you need to hand them this much. Remember that parents do the best possible job depending on their own circumstances. Try not to judge them too harshly; rather, try not to judge them at all. You yourself are/will eventually become a parent, and the experience of parenting may throw light on many of the things you resented as a child or still resent.

3.a. That was quality time your parents shared with you. You probably dropped off to sleep amid the murmur of a loving voice and mental pictures of those great stories. What made them great was not their literary quality but the fact that, read or narrated by a parent, they conveyed safety, warmth, and company. You probably looked forward to bedtime, as you knew the hassles of the day (a quarrel with your best friend, an injury from a bike fall, for example) would go away as soon as your parent and you got into the magic world of fiction.

3.b. Little children tend to dread the dark. They imagine that all sorts of monsters are lurking about, ready to prey on them the minute the lights go off. It takes time and patience to persuade them that a dark room contains the same things that were already there when the lights were on. If you were "dropped" into the dark without explanations, you probably felt anguished and had a hard time getting to sleep. This may or may not have resulted in persistent sleeping difficulties. Without knowing why, many adults feel reluctant to going to bed and roam about the house/ apartment, sit in an armchair and read themselves to sleep, or leave the television on until sleep gets the better of them. If you are married or living with someone, this behavior will take a toll on your relationship. Remember that now you're an adult, and you need to acknowledge the real meaning of darkness.

3.c. This implied your parents' setting a rather abrupt limit to "your life with us" and "our privacy." You probably felt cut off and resented it. Well, it's a style of parenting, probably based on the belief that independence should start at a very early stage. Some parents are so afraid of spoiling their children through excessive permissiveness that they go to the opposite end. Read the comment on 2.c starting with the fourth sentence. It applies to this case as well.

4.a. That you were allowed to choose your friends without parental supervision (or, at least, manifest parental supervision) indicates that your parents trusted you to choose in accordance with the family's values. Such trust on the part of your parents must have made you feel self-confident and responsible. You then probably learned to make use of these personality traits for relationships you entered into later in life. You may also know the difference between friends and acquaintances, and be tolerant of yourself and others. Moreover, you probably agree that you can share certain things with some of your friends and other things with other friends, a fact that doesn't erode your love for any of them.

4.b. It is quite likely that, if your parents chose your friends, your relationship with these children/teenagers was either superficial or strained. Although your parents selected them with the best intentions in mind, perhaps they were not aware that intrinsically "good" people do not develop a friendship just because they're good. Some parents also think of the "right" friends, those whose families and social/economic standing reflect their own. Relationships based on convenience don't last long, and even when they do, there's usually something nasty about having to think of saying the "right" thing rather than what you really feel. If you accepted this manner of relationship as natural, you may have to consider how you have chosen your present friends and decide whether you have real friends or convenient social/economic contacts.

4.c. Usually children/adolescents who have no friends come from families in which friendship is not a value. These families tend to be self-contained and self-sufficient, and they may view outsiders as threats to their safety and unity. In this sense, prospective sons- and daughters-in-law will also be treated as outsiders. Unless you were able to break out of this circle at some point, you probably find it difficult to put your trust in strangers who might eventually become friends or life partners. Perhaps you put them through a number of tests to make sure that they won't disappoint you, tiring them out and making them give up on you. Then if you happen to have no friends now, just co-workers who replaced the classmates of the past, think this out.

5.a. Parents tend to do this mainly because they fear that their children may get involved with the wrong people, run risks with disastrous consequences, or lack the necessary judgement to evaluate situations. Some teenagers rebel against this while others go along without complaining. Think of how you reacted. If you rebelled openly and tried to make your parents listen to your arguments, you were showing a healthy life drive, regardless of the outcome. On the other hand, if you pretended to accept your parents' rules and then did as you pleased resorting to lies, deceit, and the occasional connivance of your friends, you're probably behaving in the same way now, only the stakes may involve really serious matters (keeping your job, your spouse, your partner, or your credibility, for example). If you did as you were told without ever feeling you wanted some more freedom, you may have developed a submissive personality that cannot defend itself from disrespect, bullying, and ill treatment. You need to look into this, for the last two cases interfere badly with healthy relationships of any type.

5.b. As an adult, you may assume that this shows the extent to which your parents trusted you. I'm afraid that it rather indicates parental detachment or indifference to what you were doing when out of their sight. Most children tend to feel consciously or unconsciously disappointed when their parents show no interest in their whereabouts, activities, and the company they keep. Many times this parental attitude leads to reckless behavior, because the child believes that "they (parents) don't care." Parents who sincerely think that a teenager can be left to her own devices and will comply with the rules established at home are overburdening their children with more responsibility than they can handle. What did *you* do that your parents never learned about? How much unpleasantness/worry/fear could have been spared if they had been more vigilant?

5.c. You were fairly warned but not persecuted. Once you were informed of what lay "out there," the choice was yours. In other words, you were not thrown out into the world unarmed. Thus you had only yourself to blame if you erred the way. However, your parents were probably willing to listen to you and help you go back on wrong decisions ("wrong" because they harmed you or made you unhappy). Of course some parents who opt for this course of action just sit back and say, "I told you so. You messed up with your eyes open; now you mend it by yourself." When this is the case, teenagers tend to feel angry and conclude that they cannot count on their parents. Well, perhaps they overrated your capacity to discern, but you must have given some signals that you could be trusted.

6.a. If this is what you did, you felt that "a house is not a home." You were probably unhappy most of the time. It is for you to decide what exactly upset/hurt you. You are likely to find that the trouble lay with your family relationships. Some families are "expulsive," insofar as they do not establish and nurture true, lasting bonds among the members. Basic care is generally provided, with perfunctory manifestations of love. You then fled to avoid the pain, but also to find/build something better. Remember what didn't work for you when you start your own family. You will still make mistakes (who doesn't?), though not the same kind of mistake that caused your suffering.

6.b. You probably come from a well-adjusted family and grew up in full possession of the tools that can help you lead a fulfilling life. Most importantly, you are able to talk about your feelings without fearing misunderstanding. Your openness will prove crucial to all other relationships you enter into.

6.c. You probably grew up in some aspects but not in others. The notions of responsibility and respect seem to have needed further development. Perhaps you were "spoiled" and overprotected as a child, but by the time this happened you were also old enough to make up your mind on this issue as you did on others. It could be said that you were "selfish" in that you didn't think of your parents' feelings/comfort. Perhaps they remonstrated with you about this; perhaps not. Unless you have since revised your behavior to others, your personal relationships may systematically end up in failure without your knowing why. Probably your parents nagged you but eventually forgave you. Other people don't tend to be so patient/understanding.

7.a. This is in keeping with answers 2b and 6b. However, if you gave different answers to questions 2 and 6, you may want to review what kept you returning home. When things don't work the way we would like them to, we tend to try our utmost to operate a change. If our attempts at changing the course of a relationship are translated into action (in this case, talking) it is quite likely that we will succeed.

7.b. Perhaps you thought that a telephone conversation was a makeshift visit, or you couldn't take time off your studies/work. Or perhaps you really didn't wish to return, even for a short time, to a home and lifestyle that made you uneasy/unhappy/depressed you. The telephone may have been a device supporting your ambivalence; that is, you felt that you weren't breaking your bonds with the home you in fact didn't miss. Although ambivalence tends to lie at the root of most of our feelings and decisions, for so we are made, we should try to fight it on every occasion. Not only does our ambivalence send off contradictory messages to others but also makes us unsure of what we really feel/want.

7.c. You may have thought that your parents would not fit into your new environment, or that they would not approve of your lifestyle, or . . . On the other hand, you may have felt that your new environment and lifestyle would have disappointed *them*. Whatever it was, avoidance only solves momentary problems, but does very little to aid a healthy relationship. If this is your way of dealing with your parents when they embarrass you (according to your perception of them, that is) or when you believe you will meet with disapproval, you will probably apply the very same strategy to your relationships. This does not help to construct lasting, solid bonds.

8.a. You definitely love your parents. Assisting them in times of trouble comes naturally to you, most likely because the ominous "debt" already discussed never haunted your mind or your parents'. You're not thinking in terms of filial duty but of natural human kindness. You would probably come to the rescue of anyone else you loved. In other words, your capacity to love has developed to the full, and in all likelihood you are loved back by those around you.

8.b. This sounds like some sort of payback. You may feel that your parents didn't invest time and/or money in you when you depended on them, so why should you do for them more than they did for you? In fact, it's not about time or money but about love. The pain of admitting to oneself that one has not been loved (which may or may not be true; again, it's your perception) wears convenient masks to lessen the suffering. As you know if you've read *Living with Stress*, we cannot change the past, but can reinterpret it to improve the present. We can also turn over a new leaf and start anew. You don't want remorse to gnaw at you if the worse comes to the worst. Even if you now believe that your feelings won't change in the face of a bad scenario (your parents losing their home, death), experience tells that you may feel miserable and guilty. "It's never too late" mostly proves wishful thinking.

8.c. Ambivalence has come back into the picture. You and your parents strayed apart at some point of your lives, but you did have something in common at one time: your relationship. It's not a matter of what you "owe" them; you need to decide whether or not you wish to help them for the sake of love. This answer indicates that you loved them once. It's up to you to draw on those apparently bygone days. If past love doesn't move you to present positive action, you probably cast off people as you discard old clothes. This might suggest that your relationships are built and kept on the basis of usefulness rather than feelings.

9.a. Your parents were and still are important in your life. You probably have/had a great relationship that contributed to shape your own idea of a family in the best possible way. You are well aware that you weren't born to and raised in a cabbage, and can establish a healthy balance between the good and bad times you shared with them.

9.b. Usually, when we prefer not to talk about someone it's because we have nothing good to say about them or because it hurts too much. In either case, if "someone" is a parent, you have a festering wound in your heart. These infections tend to spread to other areas of your social and family life with disastrous outcomes. It would be best if you could vent your feelings to your parents if they're still alive or discuss them with another, trusted relative (a friend will do as well) if your parents have passed away. Otherwise you might find yourself implementing this "mute" pattern of behavior under similar circumstances, and at some point the burden of so much pain will become intolerable.

9.c. You don't seem to feel comfortable about your parents. As can be read in Freud's *Family Romance* (1909), many children fantasize that they have been either found or "stolen" by the man and woman who claim to be their parents, but that their real parents are of royal stock or much higher economic standing and will one day find them and take them back "home." This is a normal developmental phase provided that the child grows out of it and comes to terms with reality. However, that you, an adult, try to improve on or embellish your parents' history would suggest that, deep down, the fantasy has not been completely abandoned. If this is the case, you're probably doing the same about your relationships, endowing them with qualities they don't have. Accepting and describing people as they are will save you much disappointment, for at some point the truth is bound to come out. Through constant distortion you may even fool yourself into believing your stories, with the consequent frustration brought by waking up one day to discover a different reality.

10.a. This is indeed an issue. Your society, for reasons that would take a whole volume to explore, shuns physical contact—especially among adults—except for an occasional hug or handshake. The exception is romantic/erotic love, which obviously does not apply to this case. On the one hand, you don't want to hurt your parents' feelings by asking them not to kiss you, while on the other hand you wish you could be spared the embarrassment. Kisses are not infectious; probably your parents have got carried away by the occasion (perhaps you announced to them that you were expecting a child, for example). If you could reeducate yourself and those close to you in regard to physical contact you might discover the joy of giving and receiving love in a most fulfilling way.

10.b. Very young children and people far advanced in years tend to process love much better when physical contact is involved. The former have not yet developed their language system to associate words and meanings, and the latter may have lost it/be losing it. Still, sensitivity generally works at its best in both, so this is how they find comfort and feel loved.

10.c. Coldness doesn't usually garner love. You may think that true love needs no words or signs of affection. Perhaps not to you or to those who raised you, but have you ever asked others you care for how *they* feel about this trait of yours? Perhaps the answers would surprise you. Depending on the circumstances, excessive strictness commands respect, fear, admiration, hatred, and a myriad of positive and negative responses. It rarely commands love and, when it does, it is the sick kind. An example of this is a spouse/son/daughter going out of his or her way to earn a gesture of love from someone like you.

3

The Couple

Will you still need me
Will you still feed me
When I'm sixty-four
—McCartney (co-credited to Lennon)

Although I'm referring to a traditional heterosexual couple, I guess that this chapter holds good for homosexual couples as well. After all, it's a matter of emotional roles rather than of sexual identity.

In his *Dialogues*, Plato provides an interesting theory about our yearning for a partner:

The sexes were not two as they are now, but originally three in number; there was man, woman, and the union of the two, having a name corresponding to this double nature, which had once a real existence, but is now lost, and the word "Androgynous" is only preserved as a term of reproach.

[. . .]the gods could not suffer their insolence to be unrestrained.

At last, after a good deal of reflection, Zeus discovered a way. He said: "Methinks I have a plan which will humble their pride and improve their manners; men shall continue to exist, but I will cut them in two and then they will be diminished in strength and increased in numbers; this will have the advantage of making them more profitable to us. They shall walk upright on two legs, and if they continue insolent and will not be quiet, I will split them again and they shall hop about on a single leg." He spoke and cut men in two, like a sorb-apple which is halved for pickling, or as you might divide an egg with a hair; and as he cut them one after another, he bade Apollo give the face and the half of the neck a turn in order that the man might contemplate the section of himself: he would thus learn a lesson of humility. Apollo was also bidden to heal their wounds and compose their forms. So he gave a turn to the face and pulled the skin from the sides all over that which in our language is called the belly, like the purses which draw in, and he made one mouth at the centre, which he fastened in a knot (the same which is called the navel); he also moulded the breast and took out most of the wrinkles, much as a shoemaker might smooth leather upon a last; he left a few, however, in the region of the belly and navel, as a memorial of the primeval state. After the division the two parts of man, each desiring his other half, came together, and throwing their arms about one another, entwined in mutual embraces, longing to grow into one, they were on the point of dying from hunger and self-neglect, because they did not like to do anything apart; and when one of the halves died and the other survived, the survivor sought another mate, man or woman as we call them, being the sections of entire men or women, and clung to that. They were being destroyed, when Zeus in pity of them invented a new plan: he turned the parts of generation round to the front, for this had not been always their position and they sowed the seed no longer as hitherto like grasshoppers in the ground, but in one another; and after the transposition the male generated in the female in order that by the mutual embraces of man and woman they might breed, and the race might continue; or if man came to man they might be satisfied, and rest, and go their ways to the business of life: so ancient is the desire of one another which is implanted in us, reuniting our original nature, making one of two, and healing the state of man.

Each of us when separated, having one side only, like a flat fish, is but the indenture of a man, and he is always looking for his other half.

The beauty and ingeniousness of this metaphor cannot be denied. Through myth, the ancients explained the mysteries that troubled their minds, the unanswered questions about human nature. However, as mankind matured, the questions persisted, and the new sciences attempted to give fresh answers to the old questions. We are not sure that their answers are truer than the myths, only we perhaps understand them better because they belong in the realm of psychology. Having lost our Classical culture, most of us feel more at ease with 19th and 20th century developments.

We can then safely go back to Fromm and look into a selection of his thoughts about this particular relationship. You may find some of them deeply shocking, yet realistic enough.

> The experience of separation arouses anxiety [. . .] The deepest need of man, then, is the need to overcome his separateness, to leave the prison of his aloneness.[7]

Fromm is not talking about separation between adults, but about separation from the mother, which he calls "the source of all anxiety" while Freud names it "primary anxiety", relating it to the fear of total dissolution that returns every time "the subject is confronted with a traumatic situation."[8] Thus, our search for a partner is inherent to our nature, as we are unable to bear aloneness. What sounds disturbing is that, in Fromm's opinion,

> People see the problem of love primarily as that of being loved rather than that of loving . . . [9]

---

7. Ibid
8. Laplanche, J. and Pontalis J.B.: *Diccionario de psicoanálisis* (My own translation.)
9. Fromm, Erich: *The Art of Loving.*

He tells us that humans resort to all sorts of strategies to pursue this end, which amounts to saying that we distort our personality, trying to become a mirror of what we believe the coveted "other" desires. Think about it. Could you honestly say that you never pretended enthusiasm about issues/activities that didn't interest you in the least just because your partner/prospective partner loved them? Perhaps you're behaving so even today. Leaving deceit aside as a secondary problem, anybody who takes on a false personality runs a double risk. She either plays her role so zestfully that at some point she cannot tell which the real "I" is or, if she happens to lower her guard, her true self pushes through the dissemblance and her beloved walks away. There is no telling how the deceived party will react, though one imagines she will not take the ruse kindly.

Moreover, Fromm holds a rather pessimistic view of love in the consumer society:

[People] fall in love when they feel they have found the best object available on the market.[10]

If this is true, seeking to be loved *by* the best object available results in a time bomb.

To begin with, we would be tearing one another's eyes out for the same individual available. In societies with high social mobility, the struggle for the best object available might turn into an all-out war. Even if we don't see

10. Ibid

this happening, it isn't very encouraging to think that we choose/are chosen in accordance with market quality standards. Still, these processes are unconscious, so we keep the illusion of the old-fashioned style expressed through conscious romantic feelings. We experience the joy of love (of being loved?) until one day the relationship begins to crumble. And then it crumbles some more; the partners stand on the opposite edges of a chasm that, in Fromm's words, "[is] love that falls to boredom, disappointment, antagonism . . . "[11]

We deserve better. Before looking at the other side of the coin, use the blank pages at the end of this chapter to record what you pretended to be like in order to attract/ keep a partner and the ways in which you felt your couple was disintegrating if you underwent the experience.

While Fromm feels that the stark view of love described above responds to the reality of developed societies, he also offers a heartening picture of a healthier approach to love, not without warning us that love may be infantile, mature, or immature.

Infantile love: I love you because I am loved
Mature love: I am loved because I love
Immature love: I love you because I need you
Mature love: I need you because I love you[12]

Henry James's *The Portrait of a Lady* offers an interesting example of love that is willing to give. The language Lord

---

11. Ibid
12. Ibid

Warburton uses to propose to Isabel is in keeping with the time (19th century), but the sentiments he pours out are in no way dated.

"If I were to wait three months it would make no difference; I shall not be more sure of what I mean than I am to day. Of course I've seen you very little, but my impression dates from the very first hour we met. I lost no time, I fell in love with you then. It was at first sight, as the novels say; I know now that's not a fancy-phrase, and I shall think better of novels for evermore. Those two days I spent here settled it; I don't know whether you suspected I was doing so, but I paid—mentally speaking I mean—the greatest possible attention to you. Nothing you said, nothing you did, was lost upon me. When you came to Lockleigh the other day—or rather when you went away—I was perfectly sure. Nevertheless I made up my mind to think it over and to question myself narrowly. I've done so; all these days I've done nothing else. I don't make mistakes about such things; I'm a very judicious animal. I don't go off easily, but when I'm touched, it's for life. It's for life, Miss Archer, it's for life," Lord Warburton repeated in the kindest, tenderest, pleasantest voice Isabel had ever heard, and looking at her with eyes charged with the light of a passion that had sifted itself clear of the baser parts of emotion—the heat, the violence, the unreason—and that burned as steadily as a lamp in a windless place.

Unfortunately, Isabel rejected her suitor and later on in the story gave herself to a sinister character, a pervert and manipulator. We will discuss these manners of abuse when we come to unhealthy relationships.

The above proposal and Fromm's statements emphasize the idea that "love is primarily giving, not receiving." On the one hand, this rules out "[being] willing to give but only in exchange for receiving." On the other hand, we shouldn't misunderstand "giving" for sacrificing our selves or being deprived. Wondering what one person gives to another, he reflects that "he gives of himself, [...] of his joy, of his interest, of his understanding, of his humor, of his sadness—of all expressions and manifestations of that which is alive in him."[13] Fromm sums up his definition of mature love as "union under the condition of preserving one's integrity, one's individuality. Two beings become one and yet remain two."[14]

To us, ordinary men and women of these times, the idea of giving/loving so generously and unselfishly may sound rather puzzling. We have mostly been trained in the art of calculation. Will the chosen one be an asset to our career advancement? Will she/he fit into our social and family circle? It would be wise to find out also whether different tastes may draw us apart, and the difference between genuine compromise and lies. We often assume a false personality in order to earn the "best object available" because we don't relish the possibility of unrequited love, which is what we fear may happen if we give of ourselves

13. Ibid
14. Ibid

freely. Such fear stems from low self-esteem and lack of confidence in what makes us lovable. Rather than think of the joy of loving, we tend to speculate about the relief of being loved, to avoid the much-dreaded aloneness. Thus many couples are rooted in either infantile or immature love. If both partners settle for this, perhaps their relationship will last "till death do they part." Still, the number of separations and divorces around the world suggests that, at some point, at least one partner wants something else. We will not dwell here on noxious behaviors leading to a break-up. Perhaps the "something else" proves more of the same in a different package, marking the beginning of an endless, discouraging search. But we should give our species some credit and believe that, in a number of cases, the unhappy partner (or both) has reached maturity and realized that she made the wrong choice.

In my view, the tragedy of love lies in the fact that a) we expect to be loved exactly in the same way as we love and, b) when we come across someone willing to love us, we blind ourselves to the real person and invest her with the qualities we most cherish.

When I say "in exactly the same way as we love" I'm not talking about intensity of feeling but of manner. As no two people express their love in the same way on account of our uniqueness, either partner may feel neglected/postponed/unloved. The rather twisted yet not unusual underlying reasoning might go like this: "I never forget our anniversary. She/he always does. Therefore, the date means nothing to her/him, which shows I mean nothing."

This mind disregards that the forgetful partner has a bad memory for dates in general, and that she probably has to be reminded of her own mother's birthday, for example. But this type of relationship revolves around "me", around "the same way as I love", so unless the other partner gives up her personality to become an echo to the grumbler, the prospects look quite poor.

Suppose you tend to fall for tall, well-built, dark-eyed, well-read men. So far, none of these specimens has fallen for you. One day a medium-height, plumpish, brown-eyed, uncultivated man asks you out, indicating that he's in love with you. If you feel lonely enough, you will in all likelihood superimpose your dreamed features on him. Sooner or later the scales will fall off your eyes. Perhaps it no longer matters that your now partner doesn't physically resemble the man of your dreams. But you find his conversation unbearably dull, and you begin to wonder what attracted you to him in the first place.

Eroticism is yet another factor that may mislead us into believing that we have found the love of our lives. Fromm exalts "exclusiveness [...] loving from the essence of my being and experiencing the other person in the essence of his or her being. [...] A decision, a promise, a commitment."[15] And he goes on to explain that it "requires specific, highly individual elements which can exist between some people." Sublime words for a regrettably debased contemporary notion in which eroticism seems to have been reduced to pornography or to maneuvers taken from a "how to" handbook.

---

15. Ibid

Perhaps the phrase "the love of our lives" is just that: a phrase. But the magic it exudes drives us to a stubborn quest not devoid of purpose, for see what happens, in Anaïs Nin's words:

> In the multiple peregrinations of love, Sabina was quick to recognize the echoes of larger loves and desires. The large ones, particularly if they had not died a natural death, never died completely and left reverberations. Once interrupted, broken artificially, suffocated accidentally, they continued to exist in separate fragments and endless smaller echoes.[16]

These echoes and fragments of experience should help us recognize love and desire and reject makeshifts.

In a nutshell, choosing a partner for the wrong reasons doesn't seem a good idea. Use the blank page/s at the end of this chapter to write down how you chose/choose your partner/s and what you expected/expect from your love relationship/s. Ask yourself if you think of people (yourself included) as "an object" of love.

We will now take our leave from Erich Fromm remembering that "love is an attitude, an orientation of character which determines the relatedness of a person to the world as a whole not toward an "object" of love." Thus we love one in everybody, and everybody in one, or else we don't love at all.

Looking into more formal issues, it worries me that

---

16. Nin, Anaïs: *A Spy in the House of Love.*

the contractual aspects of marriage weigh heavily upon developed societies. I don't mean just the financial provisions of the contract, but the vows of lifelong fidelity and mutual care. Perhaps these vows made more sense when they were first written, considering that life expectancy was much shorter than it is nowadays. I have nothing against such noble promises, only reality rubs it in my face that thousands of people all over the world make one or more fresh starts and repeat these same words every time. The question in the epigraph—the title and chorus of a popular song—expresses concern for the couple in their elderly years. The husband would like to believe that they will stick together; interestingly, he wants to make sure that he will be needed, and volunteers a list of everything he is ready and willing to do if she "says the word" for him to stay with her. Away from philosophy and psychology, in very simple words, this song somehow insists that "I need you because I love you" and that the important thing is giving.

Many couples celebrate their golden wedding anniversary. Probably their relationship has gone through many phases and their love style has changed over the years; probably, too, the key to their staying together is mutual tolerance. In our frantic world, we tend to the opposite, because there seems to be little room for anything but what *we* fancy, what *we* need, what *we* expect. Sometimes our spouse, once the passion has subsided, becomes an appendix. Depending on usefulness, we keep her or dump her. New flames shine bright around us. Why not try them? Why not, indeed, if our tolerance has been stretched to the limit? Still, what is the limit? Where did the vows go?

Let me tell you an old Chinese legend about the goddess of marriage. According to the story, the goddess of marriage ties one end of a red ribbon to every newborn and the other end to another, who may or may not have been born in the same year. Failed love relationships are due to the fact that, with so many people on the planet, the ribbons get entangled all the time. Still, sooner or later the two people at the end of each ribbon will meet and find happiness together. The trouble is that some impatient people grab a blade and cut themselves loose, after which they drift along in search of a "better half" that will now be very difficult to find.

This is a good moment to reflect on your couple difficulties. Perhaps some of them go back a long way, and you became aware of them before you two decided moving in together/getting married. If you thought that you would persuade your partner to change attitudes/behaviors, you need to know that all changes start from within. Thus, unless your partner acknowledges the need for change and does something about it, things will go in pretty much the same way.

Most difficulties stem from lack of communication. This clouds all types of relationships, but it can lead to extreme frustration in the particular case of the couple. Irvin Yalom tells us that significant problems arise in relationships when people don't express their feelings. In the face of a mute/monosyllabic partner, the other never knows how she feels, besides feeling burdened by having to generate all the affect in the relationship. Yalom also warns us that, although some people believe this is not their case, they may be disguising monologue as dialogue, and that we should listen in earnest, leaving aside stereotypes and anticipations.

It's worth exploring some of the modes of verbal exchange in a couple. These modes tend to become fixed into patterns, so we wouldn't be wrong in thinking that the couples who stick to a particular kind of exchange feel it works best for them.

Let's take a couple that "talks." I'm thinking of people in their late thirties to their mid-forties who both go out to a job and have been together for some ten/fifteen years. You can raise or lower the age and the period of cohabitation, for it won't make any difference. In my example, the first exchange takes place at breakfast on a weekday. Cup of coffee in his right hand and newspaper in his left, he tells her of the hard day he will have at the office in disconnected sentences, since part of his attention is going to the paper. She makes appropriate sounds to indicate she is listening (oh, gosh, really, etc.) and takes advantage of his breaks in speech to mention that she will be working late, that the telephone bill is due today so could he please take care of it, and that her car may need overhauling. The second (and last) exchange takes place at 10.30 p.m. She comes into the bedroom where he's watching TV, gives him a perfunctory kiss, begins to undress as she runs down an office mate, and asks if he's remembered to pay the bill. He kisses her back, tells her she's blocking the screen so could she please move to the right, grunts yes, he's paid the bill, and announces that tomorrow he'll take her car to the mechanic so she'd better leave in time to catch a train. She snuggles up beside him and soon the TV is off and the couple asleep.

These people are convinced that they talk when in fact they seem to be holding an informal board meeting. Feelings are not even hinted at, and even if one or both were to ask, "How was your day?" the answer would probably be a polite "good" or "as usual." If the day was rotten, why worry the other, who probably has his/her own work problems? And if it was a great day, why make him/her feel that one is making headway while the other seems to find it difficult to improve his/her work situation? So neither of them opens up, neither asks significant questions, and they both probably refrain from doing so because they "anticipate" that things could get ugly. Neither is ready to put up with an emotional outburst, positive or negative. This type of exchange that they have kept up for years deludes them into believing there's nothing wrong with their communication, and yet they have estranged themselves from each other all along.

Now we can take a peek at a couple in which one of the partners is really extroverted. Because women tend to be accused of being chatterboxes, I will make the man "talk." He speaks assertively about every subject on earth, from daily events to economy to politics, occasionally inserting "right?" or "okay?" to make sure that he's getting his wife's/ partner's undivided attention. Which he isn't for she simply nods or offers a voiced indicator that she's listening when in fact her mind is miles away. Not that he actually cares, for he loves the sound of his own voice. This is an extreme form of monologue disguised as dialogue, yet this couple is also convinced that they "communicate."

It is most important that verbally expressed feelings—

how the other feels—mediates the relationship. Never mind if sometimes expressing one's feelings leads to an argument. As the saying goes, a good quarrel clears the air. If the partners speak out and truly listen, they are quite likely to reach the state of "two beings become one and yet remain two."

Curiously enough, some couples seem to communicate only when they quarrel, so they quarrel all the time. Parents pass on modes of communication, like so many other things, so if you inherited the quarrelsome style, it would be good to ask yourself whether this is what you would like for your children.

On the other hand, there are couples who would go to any lengths to avoid an argument, let alone a big quarrel. They may fear that one thing will lead to another, and that painful, long-hidden truths will come out that cannot be taken back. Yet even these should be spoken, if only to place our essence level with love.

Consider this beautiful, moving speech by Birkin, a male character in D.H. Lawrence's *Women in Love:*

> Because I don't know what I want of you [. . .] I deliver myself over to the unknown, in coming to you I am without reserves or defences, stripped entirely, into the unknown. Only there needs the pledge between us, that we will both cast off everything, cast off ourselves even, and cease to be, so that that which is perfectly ourselves can take place in us.

This couple (Birkin and Ursula) had a very rough time together, but they never ceased to communicate. They hurt and healed each other; there was nothing ideal or idealized about their relationship. Precisely because they were so close even in anger they were able to stay together. However, if you wish to part ways with your partner, you still need to communicate so as to make the separation less traumatic and bitter. What if your partner refuses to see sense? We will discuss this in the chapter about communication.

In the meantime, use the blank page/s at the end of this chapter to record your communication patterns.

WHAT DID YOU PRETEND TO BE LIKE IN ORDER TO ATTRACT/KEEP A PARTNER?

WAYS IN WHICH YOU FELT YOUR COUPLE WAS DISINTEGRATING BECAUSE OF DISSEMBLANCE

YOUR EXPECTATIONS REGARDING YOUR LOVE RELATIONSHIP/S

YOUR COMMUNICATION PATTERNS

4

Friendship

Friends will be friends
Right till the end
—Freddy Mercury

Now friendship may be thus defined: a complete accord on all subjects human and divine, joined with
mutual good will and affection. And with the exception of wisdom, I am inclined to think nothing better
than this has been given to man by the immortal gods.
There are people who give the palm to riches or to
good health, or to power and office, many even to
sensual pleasures. This last is the ideal of brute beasts;
and of the others we may say that they are frail and
uncertain, and depend less on our own prudence than
on the caprice of fortune. Then there are those who
find the "chief good" in virtue. Well, that is a noble
doctrine. But the very virtue they talk of is the parent
and preserver of friendship, and without it friendship
cannot possibly exist.

These are Cicero's reflections on friendship, written because he deemed "that the subject seemed one worth everybody's investigation." In his day (106 BC–43 BC) friendship was valued above other positive affects. I'm afraid that it has gone down in the ranking since then as men turned their mind and efforts to the rat race for individual success. Perhaps it would be in order to remember here that when rats run they trample on the bodies of those before them, so the ones who eventually come to their destination do so at the expense of a considerable string of dead bodies. In the human rat race, the "dead" tend to be people, no sooner cast off than forgotten the minute status seekers achieve their goals.

In ancient times friendship was cherished and honored and it still is in small present societies; however, I wouldn't like to be unfair to the predicament of large city dwellers. Perhaps we should make a distinction between newcomers to the city, people who arrived in search of better prospects, leaving behind friends and family, and natives of our megalopolis, raised in a completely different environment. The inhabitants of small towns have plenty of opportunities to make friends, but their decision to transfer to the big city generally entails severing bonds of friendship for a number of reasons. To begin with, distance and infrequent communication estranges both parties from each other. Besides, the migrant will probably acquire the more sophisticated ways of her new place of residence, and may now view her friends of yore as "primitive" men and women with whom she cannot share thoughts and experiences because they wouldn't understand her lifestyle. On the other hand, the city native's idea of friendship may be rather superficial, not because deep down she wouldn't value a soul mate but because in the rush of her life (and of the people she meets) there's no time for profound relationships, exception made for a life partner. Thus, what migrant and native usually have in common is a large, high-rotation number of acquaintances or occasional "friends," none of them committed to the relationship as real friends are.

In Australia there is a sculpture by John Robinson called *Bonds of Friendship*. The artist says that, to him, the best representation of friendship he could think of is "a chain with only two links, locked so tightly together it is inseparable, thus able to withstand all the pressures of life."

We often mistake social and work relationships for friendship, probably because we share interests with the former and many hours of our day with the latter. Still, the two parties involved at either end carefully conceal the least amiable aspects of their personality, their frustration, anger, disappointment, fears, worries and the like lest the "friend" might shy away from them. Ultimately, we "prepare a face to meet the faces that you meet"[17], a mask that, in preserving others from our dark sides, also preserves—or so we believe—our relationships.

There are those who would agree that keeping our problems to ourselves shows our care for our "friends." Yet we don't only stifle the bad things, but also the good ones. Our joys and happy moments, if not visible in the environment

---

17. Eliot, T.S.: *The Love Song of J. Alfred Prufrock.*

that we share, remain a secret to be disclosed when life forces us to admit that, for example, we have got engaged/ are getting married, have been promoted or (in the case of women) are pregnant.

Why do we tend to behave like this? I would venture to say that in our soul of souls we *know* that our acquaintances/ co-workers/neighbors are not friends. This doesn't mean that they don't care about us to different extents, depending on their own personality style and personal circumstances. However, since we have not walked the long, sometimes difficult path of friendship together, theirs is a different status, and so is ours in regard to them.

In his book *On Friendship*, Raymond E. Pahl warns us not to mistake the gang, popularity, or the peer group for friends. He also says that difficulties in making friends during childhood and adolescence may seriously impair our ability to make friends in our adult age. I'd like to add that in the developmental stages of our lives our parents/nuclear families are largely responsible for the ways we approach friendship. If our formative role models haven't shown us what friendship means through their own relationships, we will possibly have no clue to how to engage in friendship and, what is worse, may honestly believe that real friends will not actually enhance our lives.

If this is what you feel, you couldn't be more wrong. When all doors slam in our face, when our family relationships don't work the way we would like them to, when we sense that our parents and/or siblings have become strangers, when we are drowning in sadness, we need friends—a friend. You may wonder whether I'm saying that a friend and a handkerchief to wipe your tears amount to the same thing. Of course not. When "all the trees are green and every goose a swan"[18], when you experience the full joy of living, your friends, in reflecting your happiness, will act as magnifying mirrors to extend your well-being in time and to remind you of these ineffable moments when "all the wheels run down."[19]

Before moving on, use the blank page/pages at the end of this chapter to list your friends, when and how you met them, and what makes you feel you're friends.

A close friend is a blessing. Several close friends are a treasure trove. Friendship is a weft of shared experiences, mutual trust, open-mindedness, care, love, understanding, disinterestedness, and constancy. It is to be there for the other knowing that she will be there for you. Close friends are not to be taken for granted, and cultivating them entails commitment to the relationship. Since these are the friends who will laugh and cry with you, the ones to whom you can confide your most secret thoughts and feelings, it is worth investing time in friendship. Many people shy away from the kind of proximity involved in close friendship for fear of disappointment or betrayal. Perhaps they have undergone such experiences and would rather not try again. If you are one of these people, think that there may have been an initial flaw in the choice.

---

18. Kingsley, Charles: *Young and Old*.
19. Ibid

You may remember the above paragraph from *Living with Stress*, the first book of this series. Let's go over your choice of friends. To begin with, the choice should be mutual, unselfish, disinterested, and based on empathy. We have all experienced situations in which we have been attracted to people we would like to make friends with but have found no reciprocal desire on their part. Conversely, we have also been approached by people whose friendship we neither seek nor wish. Without initial empathy it doesn't seem a good idea to insist. What, exactly, is empathy? According to the *American Heritage Dictionary of the English Language*, "identification with and understanding of another's situation, feelings, and motives." The question that arises now is, how can anyone understand another person when these two have just met? Moreover, "understanding" implies rational brain activity rather than feelings. So perhaps in the context of friendship we should resort to a meaning of empathy shared by the society out of the dictionary: the perception that we could eventually identify with and understand someone's situation, feelings, and motives if given the chance to do so. Some just simplify the matter by speaking of "the right vibes."

Supposing you are the kind of person whose friendship is much sought, but you're aware of whom you want for friends, you need to put off those in whom you're not interested in the best possible way. The tenet that "honesty (the truth) is the best policy" does not seem to hold good here. Unless there are very good reasons for doing so, telling people to their faces that you don't want to be friends with them is blunt, thoughtless, and cruel. Hurting others will probably turn them into enemies, which is not what you need. Polite avoidance strategies (refusing invitations because of previous engagements, being too busy to share time/activities with them, etc.) will gently convey the message. Still, sometimes you do engage in friendship because, at first sight, the other person appears to be the right friend for you. As time passes, you discover you have made a mistake. If the other person has not intentionally deceived you, in which case you would be right to confront her, you can just drift away from her life without causing unnecessary pain.

Unlike other relationships we have discussed, friendship involves emotional exchange and unconditional mutual commitment. Giving everything of you for nothing in return makes you feel used, debased, and stupid. Then it would seem that, first and foremost, friends should have the same outlook on friendship itself. In the quotation that heads this chapter, Cicero goes farther: "a complete accord on all subjects human and divine." Perhaps this is asking too much. Besides, a friend whose points of view on certain things differ from ours will help us enlarge and enrich our own. A close friend may be indulgent to your flaws, yet not an accomplice to your wrongdoings. She functions as an ancillary memory, conscience, mind, and sensitivity. All this develops through time; close friends do not come "programmed in a package."

I'd like to share with you two personal experiences by way of illustration to the above thoughts. The first started in elementary school, when an extroverted, bright-eyed eight-year old brunette who sat a few desks away from mine came up to me during the long morning break and invited me to play at her place that afternoon. I was an only daughter (think of the connotations) and a shy child. The invitation took me by surprise, for my relationship with my classmates was practically non-existent. My "friends"—i.e., the children I dutifully played with—were the children of my parents' friends, and I didn't look forward to these "play sessions" because I had nothing in common with my playmates.

The vivacious brunette jotted down her name, address, and telephone number on a sheet torn off a copybook, thrust it into my hand, and rattled on about her mom having said it was okay and how much fun we would have until the bell rang to go back into the classroom. I barely had the time to mumble I would have to ask *my* mom. As it turned out, my mom had been rather concerned about my not making friends on my own initiative (though this had not been precisely the case), so she enthusiastically phoned Norma's mother to arrange the details. Norma was—still is—my opposite in many more aspects than she was my equal. She extracted fun from everything, had a most vivid imagination to invent games, and talked my head off. That first time she encouraged me to humor her, but didn't overlook to ask what I liked doing. My answer must have astonished her: I only liked reading . . . at eight! We grew into best friends. For over fifty years now she has given me of her joy, her dreams, her optimism, her trust in my judgment, her love of life, and so much more. I have given her of my sense of timing, my company, my analytical mind, my flexibility. . . . We have shared great times and terrible times, listened, and offered advice and comfort to each other. When I was living abroad we exchanged weekly letters so that nothing one of us was experiencing was lost to the other. We have taken care of and cultivated our friendship on the basis of unwavering loyalty, truthfulness, and love. If I now feel hopeless about something that filled me with hope before, she reminds me of my apparently forgotten views and asks me what has changed; I do the same for her. We know each other's most secret thoughts, and it never embarrassed either of us that the other was aware of the darker, more disquieting aspects of her personality because we listen, try to understand, and never judge, even if we don't agree. I started writing very young, and used to crumple my writings into a ball and throw them away. As an adult, at dinner in Norma's home, I once regretted having done so. She got up from the table, went out of the dining room and returned with a folder that she placed in front of me. The lost writings, which she had smoothed out to the best of her ability, were carefully glued to neat fresh sheets. Need I say more?

The second experience dates back to a couple of years ago. I had met my newest friends at least fifteen years before, and didn't believe that one could make close friends in advanced middle age. However, life proved me wrong, and I'm thankful for it. A guest lecturer in Spain, I happened to meet a friend who was boarding with an elderly Andalusian lady. True to the proverbial Spanish hospitality, my friend's landlady sent me a note asking me to tea. I was in two minds about accepting the invitation, but finally decided to give myself the chance of meeting her. Ninety-year old Alba looked her age, but had the sharp mind and appetites of a much younger person. She wanted to know about my country, family, and activities as she volunteered snatches of her fascinating life. She was a descendent of the great poet Federico García Lorca and wrote beautiful poetry herself. She encouraged me to visit her often, and by the end of my stay we had become very close. Because she never learned how to use a computer, we keep a regular correspondence in longhand. It saddens me that this particular friend may leave me soon, though her warmth and love will stay with me forever.

In a way, friendship calls for a far more delicate balance than other relationships. You need to be aware that someone bent on imposing her views, will, whims, and convenience on you is not your friend. Someone who clings to you when she feels dejected and depressed to disappear the minute her prospects improve and then comes back the next time she needs support is not your friend. Someone who blurts out whatever is going through her head but has no time to listen to you is not your friend. Nor is your friend someone who systematically borrows clothes and books from you and forgets to return them, loses them, or passes them on to another friend assuming that you won't mind. In regard to borrowing, the hardest issue to handle is money. If you're able and willing to lend, brace yourself up to accept that you may never be repaid, and that you will not bear a grudge to your friend on this account. Unless you're convinced that the money you lend will not raise an insurmountable barrier of ill will between you and your friend, it's probably best to refuse the loan. Your friend will understand. If she doesn't, you two obviously hold very different views on friendship.

Perhaps you have the kind of would-be friends described above. You may stick around them with your eyes open, knowing what to expect and not complaining when it happens or, if you really feel for them, you may try to explain that the game is not even. There is a remote chance that the relationship may take a different turn. The trouble lies in the fact that most of these friends' personality types drive them to behave as they do, and one wonders whether they would agree to make some introspection. Remember that all changes start within, so they will make the effort to reconsider their part in the relationship only if they don't want to lose you.

The most sensible advice about how to move about in a world in which everyone is, in principle, a stranger, was offered by Polonius to his son Laertes on occasion of the youth traveling to France:

> [. . .] And these few precepts in thy memory
> See thou character. Give thy thoughts no tongue,
> Nor any unproportioned thought his act.
> Be thou familiar, but by no means vulgar.
> Those friends thou hast, and their adoption tried,
> Grapple them to thy soul with hoops of steel;
> But do not dull thy palm with entertainment
> Of each new-hatch'd, unfledged comrade. Beware
> Of entrance to a quarrel, but being in,
> Bear't that the opposed may beware of thee.
> Give every man thy ear, but few thy voice;

Take each man's censure, but reserve thy judgment.
Costly thy habit as thy purse can buy,
But not express'd in fancy; rich, not gaudy;
For the apparel oft proclaims the man,
And they in France of the best rank and station
Are of a most select and generous chief in that.
Neither a borrower nor a lender be;
For loan oft loses both itself and friend,
And borrowing dulls the edge of husbandry.
This above all: to thine ownself be true,
And it must follow, as the night the day,
Thou canst not then be false to any man.[20]

It is unbelievable that a character that commands no empathetic feelings from an audience may have uttered such words of wisdom. However, if we were to live by these sentiments even today, our passage through life would prove infinitely less painful.

---

20. Shakespeare, William: *Hamlet.*

WHO ARE YOUR FRIENDS?

WHEN AND WHERE DID YOU MEET THEM?

WHAT MAKES YOU FEEL
YOU ARE FRIENDS?

5

It's All about Communication

Talk to me, talk to me,
Am I doing this right?
—George Nozuka

Bret Easton Ellis's *The Informers* is a collection of short stories whose characters the author himself called "frightening" in an interview with *Time Out*. What I find scary and creepy about the creatures wandering through the stories is that they speak but do not communicate. You are presented with mothers, fathers, youngsters who seem to have shared much in life and others who are meeting for the first time. Besides their grim, cynical view of practically everything, what these imitations of people have in common is that they do not wish to communicate. It's not a personality flaw but a choice. They hang out together in self-imposed isolation. Consequently, the "relationships" in which they engage are mirages. They know, but do not care. Feeling misunderstood or not understood at all is a great excuse to sustain that life sucks.

What is even creepier is that such people actually exist. In all likelihood, if asked whether they have heard that things could take a turn for the better through communication, they'd shrug and/or send you packing.

I guess you think differently. You probably want to enhance your relationships in the awareness that love lies at the foundations but needs to be expressed in all its hues, including negative feelings such as anger and disappointment, which you wouldn't experience unless love was there first.

Neuro-Linguistic Programming (NLP) established that we tend to leave out whole chunks of thought in our discourse, and posited that deleted ideas, feelings, etc. should be re-introduced into the language chain to grant that meaning will be fully apprehended.[21]

I agree that we can make a conscious effort to say as much as possible, although we have to reckon with the limitations posed by the unconscious. It will often speak by itself through slips of the tongue, for example, or will make us forget something crucial to our intended communication. On the other hand, it is true that our body can and does communicate our feelings at one given moment. Still, we need to engage in reciprocal verbal exchanges to fully convey our thoughts to others, or else we may send off and receive equivocal messages that end up by straining the relationship.

There is another, most useful approach that takes a different stance from NLP. Developed by Canadian psychiatrist Eric Berne in the nineteen-fifties, Transactional Analysis

21. For further details about NLP, see *Living with Stress* in the Bibliotreatment Series.

(TA) derives its name from the notion that every unit of social intercourse is a transaction.

Berne noticed that along a chain of transactions (a conversation/discussion/argument) there were changes in facial expression, vocabulary used, gestures, posture, breathing, etc.

Incidentally, most narrative fiction records these changes, for writers are careful observers of reality.

> 'Would you like to go upstairs now?' he asked her, in a strangled sort of voice.
> 'No! Not here! Not now!' she said heavily.[22]

You yourself recognize similar features in your own exchanges, though you probably attribute all of them to the situation under way. TA offers a different explanation that you may find useful to evaluate discourse.

In some way, TA followed into the footsteps of Russian neuropsychologist Alexander Luria, who discovered that stimulation of certain areas of the brain brought back chunks of language that the subject of the experiment reproduced while unable to endow them with meaning or associate them to some past event.

TA maintains that we are non-stop "recording machines." Up until age five, give or take a year, our brain seems to record, verbatim, events, people, times, places, feelings, and words spoken to us or in our presence. The changes that we undergo during a transaction respond to the unacknowledged

---

22. Lawrence, D.H.: *Lady Chatterley's Lover.*

playback of such recordings. We don't consciously remember "having been there before." We simply relive/enact the past under a present stimulus. When this happens, we have been transported to another dimension. We believe we are communicating with our interlocutor but are in fact either speaking to someone who's not there or repeating words spoken by someone else on another occasion.

You need a little more feedback before putting yourself to the test and finding out the extent to which this is true of you.

TA posits that three "characters" inhabit our minds: the Parent, the Child, and the Adult. The names shouldn't be taken to the letter, for they are metaphors of our recordings.

The Parent stands for everything our parental figures said and did in front of us before we acquired the basic rules of our native language. We assimilated what was done and said in our presence as a corpus of raw data composed of pleasant or unpleasant sounds and body language. Most of the data is related to rules and opinions (perception of the world) that we tend to "replay" later in life. You suddenly may find yourself involved in an exchange like this:

Interlocutor (friend): Would you like some wine?
You: Are you nuts? You can die if your drink wine
    after eating watermelon.

You never saw such a thing happen. You didn't even hear of it actually happening. And yet you're convinced it's true. Obviously, this kind of data needs examination, confirmation/disconfirmation, and updates. You utter these remarks automatically—we all do—but unless you make sure this is *you* speaking, you will be giving the wrong impression and then wondering why this friend (perhaps everyone with whom you have a relationship) doesn't take your opinions into account. The Parent takes the lead every time you pass automatic judgement without analyzing your present reality/other people's circumstances. You can also recognize her in yourself/others through uncalled for severe facial expressions, "colored" words (qualifiers), absolute words (never, always, everyone, no one) and advisory sentence openings (You'd better, if I were you, etc.) when no advice has been requested.

Just as your Parent recorded what was going on around you, your Child recorded changes/expansion of your inner world following what you saw/heard. Without the possibility of rational comprehension, the child that you once were recorded parental approval/disapproval in the face of certain behaviors. After repeated rebuke for, say, sucking a toy, the child will refrain from doing so, for she (we know this already) wants to be loved. A child cannot understand that disapproval doesn't necessarily mean lack of love, so she will probably repress all behaviors that are concomitant with parental stern faces or angry tones of voice. Because she cannot establish a cause-effect connection between her behavior and parental reactions, the child tends to believe that every negative attitude on the part of parental figures is exclusively her fault. Daddy may have had a lousy day at work and is in no mood to play this evening. He looks sullen and distracted. The child senses she's to blame. Conversely, the child also "stars" in moments of absolute bliss in which she may or may not be actually involved. When incomprehensible uncertainty/fear/excessive pressure/elation about what's going on appears in adult life, the internal Child tends to surface. You can recognize her through body language such as lip biting, pouting, a tearful voice, nervous laughter, etc. and through an excess of superlatives, complaints, and "I want," "don't want," "don't know" . . .

See if this sounds familiar:

> Interlocutor (wife): Hi darling. Did you remember to pick up my dress from the cleaner's?
> You (husband): I have a splitting headache. Been crawling through the day to get back home.

This answer evades the question and seeks pity and "motherly" care, not to mention the hidden reproach to the wife, as if she knew how miserable her husband has been feeling and still demanded satisfaction of her own needs. It would be much simpler to say "no" and explain the reasons without dramatism. But for that to happen you need the Adult to be in command.

Who/What is this character? The part of you that can process the data, evaluate the situation, place reason above negative emotions, and produce an *appropriate* response. You recognize the Adult when the individual focuses on the exchange/problem, gives factual information and, if necessary, asks questions and offers thoughts rather than know-all or know-nothing responses.

In the two exchanges above, the Adult You might have reacted in this way:

Interlocutor (friend): Would you like some wine?
Adult You: No, thanks (if you haven't yet reexamined the connection between wine, death, and watermelons and you enjoy drinking wine).

Interlocutor (wife): Hi darling. Did you remember to pick up my dress from the cleaner's?
Adult You: Sorry, no. My head's killing me. I'll pick it up first thing tomorrow.

In the first exchange, the new answer is not insulting to your friend as, just in case you haven't noticed, you called her "crazy" and "ignorant," since according to you everybody knows that wine and watermelon make a lethal combination. In addition, your friend will have no grounds to doubt your common sense.

In the second exchange, you're now apologizing for not having fulfilled a commitment you undertook, explaining what prevented you from doing so, and offering a solution. Supposing this was the dress your wife was planning to wear that very night, it would have been appropriate and positive to suggest helping her choose some other becoming garment.

When the same problematic "internal person"—i.e., Parent or Child—is in command in both interlocutors, the exchange could go on for ever without getting anywhere, which amounts to saying that communication will never be achieved.

A Parent–Parent transaction typically leaves out reality

data, is crammed with judgmental verbalizations, and the speakers delight in laying the blame outside and/or finding fault with everything. A Child–Child transaction may well turn into an exchange between two people immersed in an inner world not shared by the other. Since neither seems to mind, it will probably not make them unhappy. The disadvantage of these transactions is that they lie outside the field of communication. People in these roles speak but don't talk.

Many couples and friends whose Parent seems reluctant to make room for another "character" will, however, describe their relationship as satisfactory. Insofar as they don't question the real nature of the relationship, they find security and comfort in "us against the world" and "the world against us."

Here is an example:

Alice and June, two middle-aged retirees, have been friends for a long time or, at least, this is how they think of each other (consider what you read about friendship in the previous chapter to decide whether "friends" applies to their relationship). They are on vacation together in a South American country. Alice made all the reservations through the Internet. Everything went just fine until they arrived at their hotel, which they chose on the basis of convenient rates, central location, and facilities advertised. On arrival, they discovered that the reception staff's knowledge of English was reduced to a couple of phrases, that their room was on the third floor by the stairs, that the twin beds were too narrow and the mattresses too thin for American standards, and that the air conditioning wasn't working. Sitting on the substandard beds, they talk.

> Alice: This is outrageous. The photos I saw showed something completely different. And these people barely understood our names, so it's pointless to complain to them.
>
> June: We've been swindled, wouldn't you say? I refused to believe that these people take advantage of tourists. Well, I know better now.
>
> Alice: You can't trust foreigners. Somehow or other, they always betray your good faith.
>
> June: It wouldn't surprise me if there weren't hot water either. And I shrink to think of what sort of breakfast they serve.

The dialogue could take on other forms as well. The interesting points to notice are that a) they believe that everyone speaks English, b) they are convinced that all that glitters (on the Internet) is gold and, c) Alice doesn't feel responsible for not having checked the truth of the offer while June doesn't blame her. The fault lies outside: foreigners ought not to be trusted/all foreigners are swindlers/they (Alice and June) are in for more unpleasant surprises (breakfast and who knows what else.) Their relationship will not suffer because of this, but if they had really talked it out, both would have had to admit that they shared responsibility to different degrees. June took Alice's knowledgability for granted, and neither of them will actually try to solve the problem as long as they can find comfort in playing "the world is against us."[23]

Although these transactions are common enough, there is another kind in which the "characters" are not complementary. This is called a "crossed transaction", and can prove equally rewarding as long as it remains unchanged throughout time.

In the Parent–Child exchange, one interlocutor will play little helpless, inexperienced kid to the other's assumed knowledge of the world and of the right thing to do in the face of every situation that may arise.

Look at the following situation and the exchange between husband and wife:

Situation: A stay-at-home mom of two children aged five and seven has kept them in today because they have a bad cold. She hasn't been able to cope with the chores *and* the children, who (in her view) seem to have agreed to behave at their very worst. When her husband arrives home, mom is a wreck, the children are crying their lungs out, and there's no sign of dinner.

Husband: Hey, kids, what's wrong? Where's mom?
Kid 1: (sobbing) I don't know!
Kid 2: (hysterical) She's mad at us!
Husband: Really? What have you been up to to make her mad?
Both kids: Nothing!

---

23. Berne maintains that adults play a number of games, some of them quite sophisticated, to unconsciously strengthen their relative positions in a transaction.

The husband calls his wife's name, doesn't get an answer and finds she's taken refuge in the kitchen, where she's listlessly staring at an assortment of vegetables on the table.

Husband: Becky, my love, what's been going on here?
Mom: Richard, it's been a nightmare since you left! I don't know what's come over the kids; they haven't given me a moment's respite. I feel so helpless! I'm so sorry; I haven't had the chance to even think of dinner. I tried, see? I took the vegetables from the refrigerator, but honestly, I can't get started. I feel like a ton of bricks landed on my shoulders. Oh dear, you must feel so disappointed in me!
Husband: (taking her in his arms) No, honey; please don't say that. I know that a couple of sick kids may be a handful. Don't worry; I'll first deal with them and then fix dinner myself. Go lie down a bit; you look exhausted.

You may think that Husband and Mom have communicated. In fact, Mom (Child) has made it clear, perhaps for the umpteenth time, that she cannot manage without her husband when the kids are around. Moreover, she has reminded him of her weakness, apologized for not having done what she knew was expected of her, and manipulated the situation to exploit her husband's protective feelings. One aspect of the husband's "Parent" surfaced to the rescue, reassured and cuddled her, and there will no doubt be a happy ending.

In real communication, this couple should have a serious conversation about their respective duties in the family and find a way to get out of their fixed roles.

When transactions occur between the Child–Adult "characters," the Child vents her fears while the Adult offers reasons and factual data to prove her wrong. On the other hand, in an Adult–Parent transaction, the Parent will turn over responsibility to the Adult for decisions that go against her deeply engrained "recordings."

Although trouble does not raise its head as long as the same character remains in command on every occasion, you need to know that, depending on the circumstances, the three "characters" rotate. Different situations "hook" our Child, our Parent, or our Adult, and since the same holds true for our interlocutor, a bad combination may bring about hapless outcomes. Unless we are aware of who's speaking for us and for our interlocutor, communication doesn't take place. It goes without saying that it would be ideal to stay in the Adult mode. This takes much introspection and analysis of your transactions. You will not always succeed, but knowing what really happened will help you stay focused. In Chapter 2 we mentioned separation and left a question unanswered: What if your partner refuses to see sense? If you can get her to think of childhood recordings and later playbacks while you go over your own, perhaps the Adults in you both will come to a mature agreement. You cannot do this for your partner/interlocutor without introspection on her part, but you will avoid being dragged into playing hurtful games. If you want to see how much pain derives from lack of communication in couples and the hurtful games they may engage in, read Edward Albee's *Who's Afraid of Virginia Woolf* and John Osborne's *Look Back in Anger.*

Still, if your communication (or non-communication) style does not bother you even if it is far from being ideal, you may wonder why change. Thomas Harris[24], a best-selling Texan psychiatrist who embraced TA after becoming Eric Berne's disciple, tells us that people want to change because they have suffered too much, because they have fallen into despair to the point of paralysis, or because they have suddenly discovered that they *can* change, a finding that opens a whole world of new possibilities. You may sense a contradiction between the first statement in this paragraph and Harris's statements about change. When I speak of a communication style that doesn't bother you, I refer to the whole range of defense mechanisms working hard to trick you into believing that "everything is all right." Such mechanisms come into play precisely because suffering and despair have reached the limit of your endurance. At this point, your choices are to succumb, pretend that you're impervious to the difficulties stemming from misdirected communication, or change. This is by far the wisest and, in the long run, the most rewarding decision.

Before moving on to a discussion of abusive relationships, use the blank page/s at the end of this chapter to decide which is your prevalent "character" and/or list down situations in which you behave like a Parent, a Child, and an Adult.

---

24. Harris, Thomas: *I'm OK—You're OK.*

MY PREVALENT CHARACTER IS . . .

I KNOW IT IS BECAUSE . . .

SITUATIONS IN WHICH I BEHAVE LIKE A PARENT

SITUATIONS IN WHICH I BEHAVE LIKE A CHILD

SITUATIONS IN WHICH I BEHAVE LIKE AN ADULT

6

Putting Limits on Unhealthy Relationships

If mommy wants to eat boiled duck,
mommy's gonna get boiled duck.
—Tom & Jerry cartoon

Unhealthy relationships generally relate to the notion of control. Through various behaviors that we will explore later on, one party tries to subdue the other—and often succeeds. In other cases, those of symbiotic relationships, two people function as one, going against "union under the condition of preserving one's integrity, one's individuality. Two beings become one and yet remain two." There is still another kind of unhealthy relationship in which one party practically throws itself under the feet of the other, as if asking to be trodden on in order to be happy.

The epigraph to this chapter needs explaining so that you can understand why I feel it epitomizes one of the worst unhealthy relationships of this kind: that of unconditional submissiveness. In this cartoon, Tom "mothers" a duckling who has become deeply attached to him. Unfortunately, true to his nature, every time Tom looks at it he goes delusional and sees it roasted, fried, or boiled, laid on a platter and ready to be eaten. Finally, Tom gives in to his drive, begins looking for recipes in a cookbook, and sets to chopping vegetables. The duckling, which never leaves his side, suddenly realizes that the pièce de résistance is none other than itself. But it lacks internal, self-protective defenses; it has delivered its whole being, its life and death into Tom's hands, and so, with tear-brimming eyes, utters the sentence "If mommy wants to eat boiled duck, mommy's gonna get boiled duck." The fact that the cartoon has a happy ending does not detract from the horror of psychological suffering experienced by anyone who is willing to be figuratively "eaten" by another party if that will make the other party happy. No real correlation between domination and submissiveness necessarily exists. This is not the realm of S&M (perversion), though we'll eventually get there. What we have is someone who has completely surrendered her love of herself (remember Chapter 1?) out of gratitude, admiration, a sense of indebtedness, or a total lack of self-esteem to volunteer as an object of the other's desires. A relationship, with its ups and downs, entails some degree of active participation on either side. What we have here is an active party and someone who has drained herself of all feelings that do not serve the purpose of pleasing the other. This is dangerous and lethal, even if the other party does not take unfair advantage of the situation. Why? Because at some point the other party will tire of interacting, so to speak, with a nonentity, and leave. And then comes the question "What have I done wrong? I would have died for her." Well, what the other wanted was the partner/friend/parent to *live* out of love/joy of life per se, not as a slavish shadow. If you fall into this category, please start to reconsider your options. Find your own reasons to live independently from those you love, admire, etc. Look around you. Look inside you. What do *you* want? When and how did you begin to behave like this? Do you feel guilty about some real or imaginary way in which you hurt/think you hurt this particular person and are trying to make amends by renouncing your life? Have you tried to communicate with the other party? As domination is not an issue in this particular case, you need to do some serious thinking about your personality traits and your self-image to reconstruct your ego. That is, resort to "plastic surgery" of the psyche. I'm sorry if this sounds hard. But you're treating yourself much worse than anyone else could.

Symbiotic relationships, though not by this name, were explained in the previous chapter. The examples of complementary transactions Parent–Parent and Child–Child and of crossed transactions Parent–Child/Adult–Child result in symbiosis as long as the roles remain fixed. Perhaps we should remember that, in biology, a symbiotic relationship between two organisms results in their mutual benefit. In human relationships, symbiosis does not tend to equilibrium. With domination and/or violence still out of the picture, one party "feeds" on the other's better judgement, knowledge, self-confidence, strength, etc., while the other increases her self-esteem by willingly providing all of the above. In Parent–Parent exchanges, both parties share an attitude to life. Because they seem to have internalized the same experiences and dictums, they echo each other's thoughts to the extent that one wouldn't be able to tell who's speaking if one couldn't identify their voices. It's quite difficult to penetrate the wall they've built around themselves, and even more difficult to enter in a relationship with only one of these parties, for they think of themselves as a unit. If you're involved in a symbiotic relationship, think of what you're missing. You're looking at the world (other people) with blinders attached to your temples. While it's wise to curtail horses' side vision so that they will not panic, it's dangerous to force humans to look in one direction only. You lose perspective, have an impoverished sense of opportunities, and know little about diversity. You function as long as the other party is there. What will happen to you if she becomes seriously ill, has a sudden change of heart (you may not believe it, but it is not totally impossible) or dies? The advantages of symbiosis don't escape me. Any of the possible roles provides comfort and satisfaction . . . inside the prison the parties have built for their exclusive habitation. You need to stop this *now*. Communicate with the other party. It's not about putting an end to your relationship, but about genuinely opening the doors to others and integrating into a larger social circle. It's about freedom and independence, which may terrify you and that's why you probably engaged in this kind of relationship in the first place. I could tell you that all unhealthy relationships stem from a seed planted in childhood, but what good would that do? You have to take action as an adult, "be your age", as the saying goes. The changes will be gradual and painless. You may begin, for example, by taking up a different activity each: a sport, an art class, etc. When you get together afterwards, you will have a lot of information to exchange. Thus your world will widen, and you will learn from personal experience that you can do things on your own, have opinions of your own, and enjoy the company of others. If the other party strongly objects, you still need to wrench yourself free. You can reason with her, to a point. Beyond that, remember that you cannot change anyone who does not wish to change.

People tend to associate jealousy with couples, although it can affect every kind of relationship. In regard to the couple, some say that a little jealousy spices the bond. The trouble is that no one knows how little is "a little," for the adjective is both vague and subjective. Moreover, the very components of jealousy tell of strong negative feelings in the jealous party, who feels that her object of love and what the object represents is being stolen from her by someone/ something else (for example, an activity, career, charity work). This person believes that she "possesses" her beloved, that her object of love is indeed an inert object, a piece of property that she has acquired for a (symbolic) price, and that everyone else sets on the "object" the same value as she does. Other people pose a threat on the exclusiveness of the relationship, an exclusiveness that the jealous party cannot forego because, with typically ambivalent feelings already discussed in *Living with Stress*, she fears that the object will suddenly come to life and make a different choice. At the bottom of jealousy lie absolute lack of self-confidence/

self-esteem, terror of abandonment, anger and humiliation at the possibility of being "robbed," and other equally negative feelings. The jealous party cannot help constant inner comparison between her and would-be rivals, all the time alternating between "I excel at everything" and "I am a total failure." Sooner or later, imaginary betrayals and the psychical struggle may lead to verbal and/or physical violence against the beloved. "Better dead than with someone else."

Marcel Proust's *In Search of Lost Time* offers a wonderful example of male jealousy in the first volume, entitled *Swann's Way* in English. Fifty-year-old Swann falls desperately in love with Odette, a courtesan in 19th century Paris whose reputation he doesn't know of until much later. Read the author's words about this love:

> It is not necessary that she should have pleased us, up till then, any more, or even as much as others. All that is necessary is that our taste for her should become exclusive. And that condition is fulfilled so soon as— in the moment when she has failed to meet us—for the pleasure which we were on the point of enjoying in her charming company is abruptly substituted an anxious torturing desire, whose object is the creature herself, an irrational, absurd desire, which the laws of civilised society make it impossible to satisfy and difficult to assuage—the insensate, agonising desire to possess her.

Swann tortured himself with feverish mental pictures in which Odette betrayed him with other men (and women).

In the ambivalent state mentioned before, he soon contented himself with a perfectly reasonable, self-fabricated explanation of her innocence, but the tiniest change in her habits threw him into a new bout of despair:

> [. . .] he burned to know whom she had been seeking to fascinate by this costume in which he had never seen her; he registered a vow to insist upon her telling him where she had been going.

He imagined that, because he desired her so much, she aroused the same passion in other men, and this drove him to possess her body and soul lest an inch of his object of love should remain outside his control.

> [. . .] since he had observed that, to several other men than himself, Odette seemed a fascinating and desirable woman, the attraction which her body held for him had aroused a painful longing to secure the absolute mastery of even the tiniest particles of her heart.

We don't know whether or not to believe in the accuracy of his observation. Naturally, he also tortured Odette with questions about her past, not daring to ask about her present just in case her answers proved both true and hurtful.

> "My poor darling, you must forgive me; I know, I am hurting you dreadfully, but it's all over now; I shall never think of it again."

False. He never stopped thinking of it, kept on wondering and rewording the questions, spying on her and peering through the thin envelopes into which she sealed her correspondence, out of an irrepressible urge to prove her a liar or, ambivalently, to prove himself wrong. Swann didn't kill Odette: he married her. At the time, that gave him the power over her that he didn't have as a lover. Not that he fared too well, but that is another story.

Irrational jealousy eventually makes the victim feel guilty. She may go into a paranoid state, watching her step all along just in case something she says or does will cause hell to break loose.

If you happen to be the jealous party, you need to ask yourself whether your feelings are justified by what your partner says/does. If this is the case, have it out with her, pointing to such aspects of her behavior that make you uncertain of her commitment to you. Also bear in mind that some men/women indulge in arousing jealousy in their partners because *they* need permanent reassurance that they're loved. This is a devious strategy caused by who-knows-what hurtful past experiences. Communication between you two will give the clue to why she's doing this, after which you can make her understand that you're not the person/s who caused her unhappiness in the first place. On the other hand, if the problem lies with you, if you see ghosts under the bed, so to speak, it would be advisable to resort to introspection and find out why you suspect that you will be cheated on tomorrow if you have no proof that you've been cuckolded so far. This demands very hard work and much patience on your side. Perhaps if you consider that you may end up losing your beloved, who will eventually find your scenes unbearable and leave for good, you will sober up and take your time to restart from a different stance. However, you need to communicate with your partner, own up to your disease, and tell her that you'll be working on it.

If you're the victim, you need to tell your partner that her behavior makes you suffer. You can also help by repeated demonstrations of how much you care for her, at the same time avoiding equivocal remarks or attitudes that you positively know will drive her mad. When you live with a jealous partner whom you love, avoid, for example, singing the praises of a co-worker of the opposite sex. Unless you enjoy provoking your partner and living through the consequences this type of remark may lead to (and if this is so, something isn't right), your best bet is showing her at all times that you have eyes for her/him only.

Family and friends can also experience jealousy. While this is normal between young siblings until they learn that their parents love them alike[25], all other situations fall into the field of pathology. A jealous friend/relative fears losing her object of love for similar reasons as does a jealous partner: mostly, a possessive personality and low self-esteem. These people tend to "shield" their friend so effectively that her other relationships drop her while new prospective acquaintances shy away to avoid unpleasant situations. Jealous friends/relatives seem to resort to strategies

---

25. Sometimes one or both parents have a "favorite" child, a fact that is perfectly understandable in the field of human feelings. What is definitely wrong and hurtful is to let the children know about it.

consisting in nagging the "object" about supposedly wrong choices, pouring insidious remarks into her ears about the dependability of others, and generally trying to persuade her that they are "saving" her from bitter disappointment.

If you belong in this category of friends, you need to ask yourself why you're doing this. You will probably find that the answer does not lie in your love for the other person, but in your insecurity. You may also discover that you enjoy being in control all the time, together with fantasies of abandonment and rejection. You're mistaking friendship for ownership. Bearing in mind what you read about friendship in Chapter 4, make an effort to give your object some credit for her judgment and the freedom to engage in other relationships, even if they turn out to be a mistake. Cain was wrong to say, "I'm not my brother's keeper." In a way, we all are our friends' keepers. If we see our friends stepping into danger, it's fair to warn them. Sometimes it's even fair to take action. But it's altogether wrong to shackle them to you.

On the other hand, it's not difficult for the would-be prisoner to read the signs. If you feel you're the victim here, try to talk some sense into the jealous party. Do not allow emotional blackmail ("All I do is because I love you"; "Can't you see how much I suffer?", etc.). Unless you see the will to change, your best option is to let go of this friend or relative, because sooner or later she will harm you more than any unscrupulous stranger.

See what happened between Shelley and Bee, two young women whose friendship was tainted by the latter's jealousy. When Shelley first got married, Bee feared that there would be no room for her in the new home. She needed constant reassurance from Shelley and her fiancé that she would not be cast off "like an old shoe"—Bee's words amid much sobbing and sulking. Indeed, the couple was true to its promise, and the three of them shared time and outings. Five years later Shelley got divorced, with Bee supporting her through the mourning period. Eventually Shelley started dating again. Bee kept reminding her of her previous "failure," which she entirely attributed to Shelley's ex-husband. However, Bee didn't get overly concerned until Shelley announced that she was marrying James, a divorced father of two. James told her in so many words that, in terms of a couple, three makes a crowd and that he expected Shelley to spend time with him and his children, without ruling out the possibility of having new babies. Nothing Bee told Shelley about the "disadvantages" of this match would dissuade her: she was in love and more than ready for a fresh start. Ten days before the wedding, Bee happened to walk past a restaurant and catch a glimpse of James and his ex-wife at a window table. She sneaked a photo of them with her cell and hastened to send it to Shelley with an "I told you so!" message.

Shelley was not jealous by nature. She supposed there must have been a good reason for James meeting his ex on friendly terms. He would probably tell her himself. So she neither called Bee back nor did she try to contact James. In the evening, James came to dinner. He spoke of a number of things but said nothing about having met his ex. When Shelley asked him where he had lunched, James answered he had been too busy to leave the office and had ordered a sandwich. Shelley couldn't believe her ears. She then and there confronted him with the photo, refused to listen to his explanations ("I didn't want to drag you into my disagreements with my ex over the children's education") and called off the wedding.

Bee was exultant. Shelley hung up on James for a full month till he understood it was over. But she slowly began to avoid Bee as well. In what would be their last conversation, Shelley told her, "Perhaps you did me a favor, but I cannot help resenting you. Every time I see you or hear your voice James comes to my mind. To free myself from James I need you out of my life."

There's much to analyze in the relationships described above. However, I would like to highlight that Bee's zeal in keeping Shelley out of harm's way (and all to herself, by the way) backfired badly.

The Spanish language has a curious expression to express admiration for other people's good qualities and achievements: "healthy envy." This is a contradiction in terms. There's nothing healthy about envy, probably one of the most destructive human feelings. It is commonly believed that envious people covet what others have. If so, envy would be the inverted image of jealousy. I maintain that, far from the desire of appropriating someone else's real or metaphorical "object," envy seeks the destruction of the object for the sake of the pain its loss will cause the happy possessor.

Many cultures firmly believe that if you're given "the evil eye"; i.e., a powerfully envious gaze, you will lose something precious to you, ranging from your health to a beloved one to your material possessions. Accordingly, even today Mediterranean societies make a point of wearing charms to counteract its effects. I wouldn't advise you to fall into superstition, but to develop awareness of those who envy you.

As you read, you may wonder what you have that may arouse envy. I'm afraid that's the wrong question. It's not what you have so much as what the envious person lacks. In a nutshell, envy boils down to profound unhappiness gone awry. It is a distorted view of the self, so that rather than try to operate a change from within, the envious person deludes herself into thinking that she can obtain happiness through another person's sorrow. Every psychological/psychoanalytic landmark has much to say about this issue. I prefer to give you three examples to illustrate the ways in which envy works.

Lily Percival, June's elder sister by two years, feels that life hasn't been fair to her. June was the apple of their parents' eyes, with Lily walking in her shadow. At thirty-five, she gets by on a dreary job and has never been blessed with a loving partner, whereas June married a millionaire in her early twenties and has since been living in the lap of luxury. The sisters' mother keeps drumming her ears with June's trips to exotic places, her expensive jewels, design clothes, and whatnot. Lily does not (consciously) envy her sister. She has come to believe that, for some reason that escapes her, she doesn't deserve better than the little she has. On one of the rare occasions in which the two of them are visiting with their mother at the same time, Mrs. Percival keeps voicing her admiration for June's new Kenzo frock, made of an exquisite fabric that seems to change color with the light. Around four in the afternoon, Mrs. Percival carries a well-laden tray into the living room. She's about to pick up the teapot when Lily says, "It's okay, mom; I'll do it. You just sit down and enjoy it, after all the trouble you put yourself through to prepare such delicacies." Lily pours her mom a cup of tea and hands it to her with a warm smile. She then picks up a cup for June. In a strange maneuver that none of them can explain, least of all Lily, the piping hot tea ends up on June's legs, which get badly burnt under the flimsy fabric. It goes without saying that the dress is ruined beyond repair. Lily felt quite miserable at her "clumsiness," but was also surprised that she worried more about having been clumsy than she did about the damage she had caused. If we went over the history of these two sisters, we would learn of other incidents pointing to this "grand finale."

June never suspected this was an outburst of envy. Perhaps you don't either when similar things happen to you. An isolated episode is an accident. A series of episodes screams envy. If you're the target of envy that is unknown to your victimizer, you need to broach the subject and *communicate*. You will probably come across horrified denial and hurt feelings on her part, for she will not readily agree that she means you harm. How could she when her envy is totally unconscious? Yet once these people are confronted with facts, they tend to resolve their ambivalence. They need help through a demonstration of love as we described it in Chapter 1. True love from family/friends proves a great cure for this kind of envy.

Now let's look at the situation from the opposite end. Assuming you're the one who feels she's not getting a fair deal as far as life goes while others seem to be carrying off all the big prizes, you need to do some introspection. I'll propose some questions you may ask yourself, and I guess you may add many others. After all, as I told you in the Introduction to *Living with Stress*, you know yourself better than anyone else does.

SUGGESTED QUESTIONS

1. Am I an envious person?
2. Whom/What do I envy?
3. In what way/s would my life change if I obtained what I envy/if I were that person I envy?
4. Have I ever obtained something I envied? If so, did my happiness last?
5. Who was the first person/thing I envied?
6. What positive action have I taken to acquire the qualities/objects that I envy other than trying to snatch them from others?
7. Do I get satisfaction through depriving someone else from her joy?

Use the blank page/s at the end of this chapter to give truthful answers. If you are a "Lily", please make sure that your denial mechanisms don't interfere.

The right path to follow is to admit that you are envious of someone in particular or of everyone you deem "undeservedly successful/happy." You will probably list a number of objects you envy, but envy, like desire, is metonymic[26]. Remember an occasion when you in fact obtained exactly the same object as the other party had. You probably felt that it was and it wasn't the same. Of course it wasn't, because you wanted *her* object. It was necessary for her to lose it and suffer for it, which didn't happen. Thus your happiness was short lived. Allow me to tell you a little personal anecdote. I used to have a colleague who was extremely generous . . . and envious, although she wasn't aware of this. On a trip together, following her advice and guidance, for she was an expert in the matter, I bought an inexpensive photo camera. She immediately found it far more attractive than her own, a German one that had cost the earth. My colleague went back to the store where we had purchased mine and bought exactly the same camera for herself. A couple of days later, she lost it. For the rest of our trip she kept borrowing my camera because it was "easier to handle" than her sophisticated German device, until one day she accidentally dropped my camera and broke it.

No alarm bell rang at that moment. Back in Buenos Aires, my colleague asked to become my student. This really threw me off my balance. What could I teach her that she didn't already know? She argued that I was a specialist in international examinations, which she wasn't, and that she was considering giving her career a new twist. She attended private tuition for a year or so, and then announced that

---

26. Metonymy is a literary trope, but in psychoanalysis it refers to the constant sliding of signifiers. Applied to desire (and this is an oversimplification, but it's all I can offer for the purpose of this book), it means that one object will systematically be displaced by another ad infinitum.

she didn't think she would ever accomplish her goal. "We've practically reached the end of the course," I said. "In a few more months you'll be ready to train your own students!" And she replied, "That's not what I meant. I wanted to take classes with you to discover what makes you so special to your students. Now I know, but I also realize that I'll never be you." Good heavens, this woman was envious of my *self*!

If you remember who/what you first envied, try to associate the moment with something that may have made you felt unloved/unhappy. When the memory comes to the focus of your mind, try to reinterpret it in the light of the circumstances and of your life experience. And then let go of it. Balance the episode against better times. Count your blessings. Try to think positive, for if you don't change your internal attitude people will eventually leave you alone, which must be one of the ghosts that haunt your mind.

You may or may not have striven to fulfill your desires without meddling with others. Perhaps you did but failed. If this is the case, consider that Rome was not built in one day, that perseverance is usually the key to success, and that you may not have wanted your "object" badly enough to earn it. If you've been too busy envying others, you've wasted stamina that you could have used to get what you desired through legitimate means. Give it a try. When envy is at stake, it helps to feel that you yourself may eventually be the envied one. In other words, you will be turning your negative envy into a positive "achieving machine."

Lastly, the satisfaction of depriving someone of their joy speaks of some kind of retribution buried deep down in the past. As you apparently cannot take revenge on the person who hurt you, you go around hurting whoever happens to be at hand. Again, try to remember who slighted you, reinterpret the facts, forgive, and let go. In the long run, hatred disguised as envy will end up poisoning you as much as it will harm your victim. The two following examples tell of this particular, lethal kind of envy.

When ordinary people set to name the central themes in Shakespeare's tragedies, they associate *Othello* with jealousy. I do not intend to offer an analysis of this most complex play, but would draw your attention to the fact that the tragedy would never have unraveled had it not been for Iago's *envy*. Othello, a moor, a newcomer to the white, highly civilized Republic of Venice, has been appointed to the highest military position and named Cassio his lieutenant. Iago believes the post should be his by right of nationality and services rendered. As if this were not enough, the black alien has earned the unconditional love of the most coveted, virtuous woman in Venice. Iago does not intend to replace Othello but to annihilate him, because only the Moor's complete destruction will bring him peace and heal the cancerous envy that gnaws at his heart and mind. We know that, in the end, Iago also perishes. How could it have been otherwise if he breathed only to envy? Iago has nowhere to go in this world once his object of envy is dead.

See the envy of the self portrayed in Shakespeare's lines:

Were I the Moor, I would not be Iago:
In following him, I follow but myself[27];

---

27. *Othello*, Act I, scene I.

Though I do hate him as I do hell-pains.
Yet, for necessity of present life,
I must show out a flag and sign of love,
Which is indeed but sign.[28]

Iago makes it crystal clear that, until the time comes to carry out his plan, he must pretend to love Othello. He speaks of hatred, and plots out of envy. Beware that when envy consciously seeks destruction of the object, the envious party hates it with all her might.

The Moor is of a free and open nature,
That thinks men honest that but seem to be so,
And will as tenderly be led by the nose
As asses are.[29]

Moreover, Iago knows human nature too well. He trusts that good men take it for granted that others speak the truth just as they do, and that no malice hides behind a kindly countenance. On this he counts to undo Othello.

that I do suspect the lusty Moor
Hath leap'd into my seat; the thought whereof
Doth, like a poisonous mineral, gnaw my inwards;
And nothing can or shall content my soul
Till I am even'd with him[30]

---

28. Ibid. Act I, scene II.
29. Ibid. Act I, scene III.
30. Ibid. Act II, scene I.

One of the most dangerous traits of envy is that, when the object seems unattainable (for the purpose of destruction), it is endowed with imaginary flaws that turn it despicable in the eyes of the envious party. In accordance with the rules of ambivalence, the envied object becomes worthless, and its very worthlessness justifies its destruction.

Thus Iago "suspects" that the Moor has slept with his wife, and wants to get even with him, only that an eye for an eye—a wife for a wife—will not satisfy him. This is but the excuse he gives himself to justify the hideousness of his plot. Envious people tend to feel that they are dispensing retribution for wrongs received.

In 1995, a thriller called *Seven* shook audiences all over the world. You may remember that the plot involved two cops chasing a serial killer who fashioned his crimes along the pattern of the seven deadly sins. What interests us is that the psycho who claimed that the world should be cleansed of sinful scum incurred the sin of envy. After being unsuccessfully tracked down, one day he walked into the police station and gave himself up. But before making a formal confession, he demanded to be driven to a certain spot away from the city, where he would provide evidence of his last crime. While waiting on the road, guarded by the two detectives, he told the younger, in so many words, that he envied his life. He envied his beautiful wife, the warm welcome he must enjoy returning home at the close of day, the love between them. None of this seemed to make sense until a van arrived with a box addressed to the young cop. As the elder detective opened it and stared in fascinated horror at the severed head of his partner's wife, the murderer calmly declared that, knowing that he couldn't have what he envied, he had killed her and now expected to be shot by the maddened husband. Hard as the more experienced detective tried to stop him, the widower emptied his gun on the psycho's body. His life was twice destroyed: he lost what he loved most, and would be tried for murder. Even if there were extenuating circumstances and he were acquitted or served a lighter sentence, his life had been stolen from him, and the murderer had achieved his purpose.

If you feel that someone in your circle envies you in this way, the best advice I can give is run for your life, literally. These people won't stop no matter what you do to appease them. It would take a thick volume of psychoanalytic theory to explain what causes them to be what they are, but you don't need an explanation, and an explanation would not save *you*. This is one of the rare cases in which communication proves useless because the wavelengths are different. This kind of envy is totally conscious, vicious, and lethal.

Manipulative behavior on the part of your relationships can seriously and insidiously impinge on your life. The worst of it all is that you willingly allow the manipulator to have her way. How can one be so naive? Easy. Unlike other dangerous people—"toxic" people they now call them—manipulators don't appear threatening to their victims. They hide their intentions behind a variety of masks ranging from the poor helpless little thing to the infirm weakling that might fall ill/die/lose her job/her home unless the chosen prey comes to their rescue.

Manipulation seeks the manipulator's own gain. It goes as far back as the Garden of Eden. You may remember this passage from Genesis:

> Now the serpent was more subtle than any other wild creature that the LORD God had made. He said to the woman, "Did God say, 'You shall not eat of any tree of the garden'?" And the woman said to the serpent, "We may eat of the fruit of the trees of the garden; but God said, 'You shall not eat of the fruit of the tree which is in the midst of the garden, neither shall you touch it, lest you die.' " But the serpent said to the woman, "You will not die. For God knows that when you eat of it your eyes will be opened, and you will be like God, knowing good and evil." So when the woman saw that the tree was good for food, and that it was a delight to the eyes, and that the tree was to be desired to make one wise, she took of its fruit and ate; and she also gave some to her husband, and he ate.

Most learned biblical scholars agree that the serpent stands for Lucifer, the Fallen Angel, who tricked Eve into eating the forbidden fruit and giving a taste of it to Adam. Lucifer's gain consisted in acquiring his share over the fate of God's creatures, whereas Eve didn't reveal to Adam her conversation with the serpent lest he should refuse to comply with disobedience to the Maker. Or perhaps she just wished him to enjoy a much desirable morsel without misgivings. At any rate, the devil manipulated Eve, and she her partner. According to the Bible, we owe all our misfortunes in the valley of tears to which the human race was confined after the expulsion from Paradise to these two manipulative practices. Whether or not you are a believer, and even if the story is a metaphor accounting for the intrusion of evil in human nature, it should suffice to beware of manipulators, but much more can and will be said here.

Basically, a manipulator uses people, though not just any people. She explores the personality traits of those around her in search of very specific responses. For example, the best preys are individuals who tend to feel omnipotent, boast of never letting anyone down, and believe they can play Robin Hood to the actual and metaphorical destitute of this world. At the other end of the spectrum, people easily given to feelings of guilt, "debtors" to anonymous creditors, and overly compassionate for their fellow beings make great targets as well.

An additional trouble lies in the fact that we tend to think well of others, particularly our relatives, friends, and respected co-workers. Thus when a little voice inside us begins to whisper that we're being taken advantage of, we hush it up, disregarding our instinct. Manipulation basically entails aggression against which you cannot defend yourself for the simple reason that you don't see it as such. Like other abusive behaviors, ultimately manipulation is about control.

In *All About Eve*, a 1950 American release starring Bette Davis and Anne Baxter, you can see how it works to a T. Margo Channing (Bette Davis) is a reputed actress with a happy private life. One evening her friend Karen ushers in Eve Harrington (Anne Baxter), a young fan whom she has found freezing at the back door of the theater, waiting to see Margo come out yet not daring to approach her over the many hours she claims to have spent there after every single show. Her admiration is so moving, her devotion so tender that great Margo first accepts small services from her and then decides to offer her a job as an assistant. Not for a moment does Margo suspect that she has been targeted as a victim. Eve secretly begins rehearsing Margo's part in a new play and persuades Karen, playing "poor little me," to keep Margo out of the way for just one performance. What wrong could it do? There's no way the inexperienced, un-trained assistant can overshadow the great star. Still, this very night, using Margo's name as bait, Eve has invited the most important critics to the theater. Her performance impresses them to the extent that she gets to play the lead in Karen's husband's new play, originally intended for Margo. Eve black-mails her way to the top, and stops short of nothing: she even steals Karen's husband from under her nose. She first makes a pass at Margo's lover, who wants nothing with her, but second best will do just fine. Because of the time when the film was shot, poetic justice knocks at Eve's door in the height of her glory under the shape of a young, devoted admirer that, as hinted by the final scene, will become her nemesis.

If this had been real life, the new girl wouldn't have stood a chance, for a manipulator can smell another miles away. These people are extraordinarily cool-headed; they seem to have trained themselves to shun emotional com-mitment. A shocking utterance by Philip, the antagonist[31]

---

31. In literature, main character in opposition to the protagonist. The antagonist is usually depicted as a villain, though not in this case.

in Irvin Yalom's must *The Schopenhauer Cure*, puts their purpose in a nutshell:

> A little friendliness and warmth makes it possible to manipulate people just as we need to warm wax if we wish to work it.

In other words, what you take as their warming up to you boils down to a carefully thought up plan to shape your will to their interests.

Eve Harrington played at making herself indispensable to her victim while doing her best to appear as fragile and vulnerable to Karen, at least until she had everyone exactly where she wanted them. However, the querulous, plaintive manipulative type can arouse such an amount of compassion and guilt in you that you will be, unawares, renouncing your very life in an attempt to compensate them for their "bad luck" or whatever they come up with in their tearful narratives.

The following is a true story that proves that the "cry wolf" fable does not usually end as its moral warns us. You may remember the shepherd that manipulated farmers to come to his aid by desperately shouting the animal's name and then laughing at their gullibility since it was just his peculiar way of amusing himself at their expense. You may also remember that he was told, "One day the wolf will come but we won't, for we'll think it's your usual joke again." And the wolf did come and had its feast.

In real life things seem to work differently. Marian, a fifty-odd widowed mother of an only daughter (Muriel) subtly and slyly discouraged several prospective sons-in-law because she felt that Muriel's role in life was to take care of her in her old age just as she had devoted "the best years of her life" to raising her child. She would welcome Muriel's boyfriends huddled in a large armchair that made her look frail and tiny, would put her hand to her heart, wince a couple of times, and say, "It's nothing" when asked if she was unwell. Naturally, the resignation in her voice belied her words. A few remarks about a "not really serious heart condition," and "I don't know how I could possibly manage without Muriel, though of course I would be the happiest of mothers if she found her Mr. Right," sent the men out the door in record time.

The day came when Muriel met Clark, who didn't shy away from her for two reasons: he was deeply and truly in love, and suspected Marian was malingering. He also trusted he would succeed in persuading Muriel to slowly take her own life in her hands. When Marian realized this relationship was for keeps, among other things she managed to give herself a heart attack the day before the wedding, which had to be called off until she recovered, and another during the couple's honeymoon. With Marian calling her in several times a week at all hours because she "sensed" the next and probably fatal attack was coming, Muriel spent more time at her mother's than at her own home. She reacted indignantly to Clark's accusations of Marian's manipulative practices and, little by little, she estranged herself from him, making things worse by refusing to have a child as her hands were already full with taking care of her mother. A couple of years later, the couple got a divorce and Muriel moved back with her mother, whose heart condition remained miraculously stable until she died of a stroke at the ripe age of ninety-two, leaving behind an embittered daughter who did her duty while hating both her mother and herself.

Tennessee Williams's *The Glass Menagerie* also touches on the issue of manipulation by a mother, although this is by no means its main theme. The complexity of the play goes far beyond the scope of this book, although it's well worth reading for the sake of the light it sheds on family relationships. In any case, the daughter remains chained to the mother and the son bolts, although the structure of the story suggests that remorse for having abandoned the two women will never stop haunting him.

What has been said so far can help you find out whether you're a victim to manipulation. What to do? Simply begin to say "no." Do not worry about hurting the manipulator's feelings; she's not taking *your* feelings into account when pursuing her agenda. A firm "no" will probably throw her off her balance and make her wonder what part of her technique failed. Very probably, she will come at you again, with variations. She will deploy a series of future personal disasters (for example, unless you help her, she may lose her job, home, husband, wife, health, or life) or will rebuke you for your ungratefulness after everything she's done for you. One thing you need to learn is never to argue with a manipulator. She's much better trained at the skill than you are, so it's a battle lost from the start. You'll end up by yielding once more, and hating yourself for it. If you care for the person, you may tell her that the game is over, and that you're willing to continue the relationship on the basis of new rules. If she cares for you, she may be ready to do some introspection and initiate a process of internal change. This is not easy, and there will be relapses. But you can help by pointing them out to her. The first step is for the manipulator to accept that she has a problem. Unless you manage to get her do this, the wisest course of action is to part ways, for the alternative solution will not work for you: you will be manipulated to the end of eternity.

It is said that low self-esteem is one component of a manipulative personality. This may or may not be so, but you cannot be tolerant of the behavior because of its roots. Every abusive attitude stems from serious psychic maladjustment; if we were to put up with them out of compassion the law should not punish child molesters, embezzlers, arsonists, serial killers, and so on. As far as relationships go, you're not a therapist (even if that happens to be your profession). Within the confined atmosphere of a consulting room, the disturbed party is a patient and should be treated as such, helped, and not judged. Outside the consulting room, we have no patients' privileges.

Now let's imagine for a moment that you are a manipulator. In a way, we all are at some time or other. You don't think so? Try to remember an occasion when you told a white lie not to upset someone whose help you needed, or pretended a headache to avoid having sex with your partner without hurting his/her feelings. . . . You can spot the episode yourself. As I stated in the introduction to *Living with Stress*, I don't know you. The only person who *really* knows you is *you*. Still, an occasional act of manipulation, though nothing to be proud of, does not make you a manipulator. It takes repeated, consistent manipulative behavior to earn the name. Supposing, then, that it has just dawned on you that you belong in this category, know that you can change. You only need to mentally reverse the roles and put yourself in your victim's shoes. How would you feel if you were constantly blackmailed/cajoled/coerced into doing things that bother you immensely lest the manipulator suffer some unimaginable loss/pain/illness? Use the blank page/s at the end of this chapter to list your manipulative tricks and what you would have felt had you been their target. Unless you're a selfish, cold, antisocial biped[32], this must lead to a sincere wish to stop taking advantage of others' kindness, weakness, or patience. And then acknowledge your wrongdoing, begin afresh, and forgive yourself. This is important. It would be ideal if you could also ask forgiveness of your victim, but perhaps this is too much to ask.

A number of other abusive behaviors cannot be understood away from the field of psychiatry and/or psychoanalysis. They derive from extremely serious pathologies which have no place in this volume, exception made of one about which I will say a few words because it tends to be mistaken for something else.

Most people believe that perversion necessarily refers to some form of aberrant sexual behavior including sadism, masochism, fetishism, and voyeurism. They believe right, except that, besides, the perverse believe that they enjoy *ownership* of the other and that they and only they know

---

32. Schopenhauer's derogatory name for human beings, as quoted in Irvin Yalom's *The Schopenhauer Cure*.

what the other wants. Accordingly, they use the other as an inert object and deny her every inkling of subjectivity. If you want to learn more about the subject, I advise you to read the Marquis de Sade, especially *Philosophy in the Bedroom*.

To put an end to the list of the most damaging unhealthy relationships, let's take a peek at sociopaths, a messy combination of liars, manipulators, exploiters, and sadists all enwrapped in an attractive package of charm and seduction.

The sociopath seems to read your mind. You will be instantly attracted to her, for she reflects, like a mirror, your thoughts, opinions, feelings, likes and dislikes. She's generally charming, has great social skills, and will make you feel that you're the center of her world. Don't let her delude you. Despite protestations to the contrary, in her sick mind *she* is the center not only of her world, but of the whole world. Basically, the sociopath feels she has the right to get everything that catches her fancy regardless of the means. She demands that you help her in her endeavors and, as happens in perversion, knows perfectly well the boundaries between right and wrong yet prefers to ignore them, as acknowledgement of moral rules might stand between her and her object of desire.

When you confront a sociopath with what she has done, she will either deny it or apologize with tears in her eyes if she perceives that she might lose your support or whatever it is she wants from you. She sounds so repentant, so willing to make amends, makes such heart-rending promises of mending her ways that you get trapped over and over again. Your forgiveness, in fact, turns you into an accessory to baseness or downright crime.

Siri Hustvedt's *What I Loved* masterly depicts the relationship between two families in which one child develops into a sociopath:

When I confronted Mark about lying to me the following weekend, he looked surprised. "I didn't lie, Uncle Leo. I changed my plans with Mom. I called Dad but they were out. I came up to New York anyway to see some friends, and then I had the key problem."

"But why didn't you tell Bill and Violet that you were here?"

"I was going to, but it seemed kind of complicated . . ." [a perfectly reasonable explanation follows]

I accepted the story for two reasons. I recognized that the truth is often muddled, a tangle of mishaps and blunders that converge to appear unlikely, and when I looked at Mark as he stood before me with his large steady blue eyes, I was absolutely convinced he was telling the truth.

"I know I mess up," he said. "But I really don't mean to."

"We all mess up," I said.

The "key problem" was that Mark broke into Leo's apartment under pretext of having lost the key to his father's (Bill's) apartment. With Leo out for the evening, he made himself at home and lay down to sleep on a bed that was absolutely forbidden to him, a bed that had belonged to Matt, Leo's only child who had died tragically at the age of eleven.

Mark's parents were divorced, and Bill had eventually married Violet. Leo, whom Mark called "Uncle", was the boy's favorite target, although he exercised his sociopathic charm on his own family as well. Yet Leo proved the weakest, since he believed that doing good by Mark brought him back to some sort of parental role that he had been deprived of by Matt's death. No doubt Mark was well aware of Leo's befuddlement about truth, half-truths, fantasies, and lies[33], and he took ample advantage of it, to the extent of luring him into a situation that nearly cost Leo his life.

If you have a relationship with a sociopath, put an end to it at once. There is no cure for sociopathy, simply because the sociopath will never admit to her maladjustment. The first step to solving a problem is acceptance that it exists. Forget that this will ever happen. You need to give the sociopath up and mourn your loss if you must, but by all means keep her out of your life. If you try to play good Samaritan to a sociopath, others who love you and whom you love may soon be grieving for *you*. Have I frightened you? Excellent. That was exactly what I meant to achieve.

---

33. I do not imply that truth is absolute but rather tend to agree with Oscar Wilde that "the truth is never pure and rarely simple." However, the accumulation of suspiciously "truthful" lies that a sociopath can produce should open your eyes provided that you want to see.

ARE YOU ENGAGED IN AN UNHEALTHY RELATIONSHIP? WRITE DOWN WHAT MAKES YOU THINK SO.

YOUR ANSWERS REGARDING ENVY

ARE YOU A MANIPULATOR? WRITE DOWN WHOM YOU MANIPULATE AND HOW.

**ARE YOU READY TO CHANGE?
WRITE DOWN WHAT YOU PLAN TO
DO ABOUT IT.**

7

Final Words

There was a jolly miller once
Lived on the river Dee;
He work'd and sang from morn till night,
No lark more blithe than he.
And this the burden of his song
Forever used to be
I care for nobody, no, not I,
If nobody cares for me.
—English folk song

You may think that I haven't told you much about how to improve your personal relationships. However, provided that you've carefully read the preceding chapters, it's all there. You now know that a harmonious relationship with yourself is the cornerstone of all successful relationships, that you first began relating to yourself and others within your family matrix, which may need correction, and that love and communication lie at the base of every successful, fulfilling relational exchange. Moreover, you've been warned of the dangers posed by unhealthy relationships and told which can be mended and which should be shunned.

The epigraph I've chosen to close this book is the first stanza of a very old song; how old we cannot say. It summarizes beautifully the happy frame of mind of a miller whose instinctive wisdom prompted him not to pine for the love or attention of those who didn't love him back.

With the passing of time, as the song was transmitted from one generation to the next by word of mouth, it underwent a number of changes. I'd like us to go over the third known version, which reads as follows:

> The reason why he was so blithe,
> He once did thus unfold;
> The bread I eat my hands have earn'd;
> I covet no man's gold;
> I do not fear next quarter-day;
> In debt to none I be.
> I care for nobody, no, not I,
> If nobody cares for me.
> A coin or two I've in my purse,
> To help a needy friend;
> A little I can give the poor,
> And still have some to spend.
> Though I may fail, yet I rejoice,
> Another's good hap to see.
> I care for nobody, no, not I,
> If nobody cares for me.
> So let us his example take,

And be from malice free;
Let every one his neighbour serve,
As served he'd like to be.
And merrily push the can about
And drink and sing with glee; [. . .]

The narrator in the song quotes the miller's explanation for his well being. It's interesting to notice that he doesn't covet the impossible (gold, in this case, but you can extend it to whatever lies out of reach). He does not owe money, loves those who love him, administrates his money wisely, lending some to friends in need and helping the poor in the modest way he can afford to, and does not feel jealous when others succeed where he has failed. The narrator then advises us to follow the miller's example, to do unto others as we would like others do unto us, and to live our lives to the full.

Why does this seem so difficult? I've been repeatedly told that "simple" people enjoy many more chances of being happy than more intelligent and/or educated people. Supporters of this theory ground their argument on the fact that the simple (in fact the word they use is "simpletons") find contentment in life as it comes without racking their brains in an attempt to find answers to the fundamental questions of existence. I couldn't disagree more. That words such as "the unconscious," "personality traits," and so on were not used and catalogued until the late 19th/early 20th century in no way means that these categories began to exist only when some enlightened thinker coined the terminology.

Basically, mankind has remained the same since at least the first recordings made by the Greek tragedians. Were Aeschylus, Sophocles, and Euripides speaking of the common man, of you and me? Not really, yet they were indeed bringing to light what ailed the common man who had not made his peace with himself. Stripped of the grandeur with which their use of language enhanced the problems, what haunts you in these times is no different from the despair experienced by the characters in the tragedies. Your modern Phaedra, in flip-flops and bleached hair, may be sitting next to you as you read. She may even be a member of your family. If we take it to an extreme, she may be *you*.

So what has changed? On the one hand, we tend to make a clear-cut separation between fact and fiction, oblivious that fiction models itself on fact. On the other hand, after reading excerpts or simplifications of the complex existential theories posited by modern philosophers and psychoanalysts—for few laymen have explored the full works—muddled conclusions about our human nature seem to have overpowered our common sense. To complicate things further, the entertainment industry has done its best to persuade us that "all is well that ends well." Thus the world seems to be divided between those who seem to find solace in "collecting" problems and those who regret having to face such problems as life drops them on their way.

The Schopenhauer Cure, a must-read by Irvin Yalom, vividly shows the process of change within group therapy. Since you're fending for yourself and your companion is this book, let me introduce three of Yalom's concepts that may help you further improve your relationships.

You have read about the need for love and real communication. Yalom advises to listen more. Indeed, any real exchange should be based on listening attentively to the other party rather than on solely focusing on what you have to say. Listening will give you an understanding of what the other feels, wants, needs, resents, and wishes to convey. Listen to the way your interlocutor structures her language; above all, listen beyond the language. Remember that we communicate both through verbal and body language, and beware that sometimes one of these languages belies the other. Listen with your ears, but use your eyes as well and remember that even then your perception will process the information in accordance with your particular vision of the world. In other words, do not react automatically to what you think you hear. If necessary, ask about what seems unclear to dispel your doubts.

Yalom also says that people cannot give what they don't have. This seems to be a major obstacle in relationships, as we tend to ignore the uniqueness so often discussed in this series. Once a subjective structure has been shaped, it will work with its constituents, expanding them, enriching them, and multitasking. Sometimes we seem to lack certain feelings that are buried deep down because of traumatic experiences or other reasons. These can resurface given time and intensive personal searching. But what is not there cannot be glued or "orthopedically" attached to the subject. Do not ask for more than the other party has to give, for by the same token *you* cannot give more than you have. If you cannot accept what is lacking in the other, you're either excessively demanding or this is the wrong other. Yet some people find it so difficult to let go of their fixation in one particular other that they either endow her with what she doesn't have and live a blissful delusion or waste a lifetime stubbornly trying to inject the missing trait/s. This is cruel to both. Do not seek the perfect match in love or in friendship or family. Measure what the other has against what she doesn't have. See what way the scales tip. And make your decision.

The third and last concept warns us against being "role-locked lest we continue to be perceived as the same person."[34] Yalom means that even after we have changed, we may keep the attitudes that defined us before the change, which obviously prevents others from noticing that we are no longer the same person.

I'd like to extend the notion of roles to other aspects. We all play multiple roles insofar as we are daughters/sons, parents, bosses, employees, co-workers, siblings, friends, customers, and so forth. Sometimes, because we spend more hours at one role than we do at others, the mannerisms of this role stick with us at inappropriate times. I remember an incident that took place after endless hours marking papers at school. Seeing that she would not get home in time for bathing and feeding her children, a colleague phoned her husband and said, "Kevin, you must give the kids their bath, have dinner with them and put them to bed. Have I made myself clear? Okay. Now repeat."

---

34. Yalom, Irvin: *The Schopenhauer Cure.*

After a few seconds she hung up and went back to her stack of compositions. One of us felt compelled to ask her if she had listened to herself talking to her husband. Our colleague looked up in surprise. "What d'you mean?" she asked. "You talked to your husband as if he were one of your not very bright students," said the one who had dared point this out. "Really? I guess that's the way I talk," answered the busy teacher.

This marriage ended in divorce. There were probably other issues between them, but I reckon that no spouse relishes a partner fixed in the wrong role. Flexibility and speed to get into the right role has preserved many a relationship.

There's a last contribution I'd like to make to the improvement of your relationships: a beautiful poem with a peculiar history. Believed to have been found in a Baltimore church in the 17th century, *Desiderata*[35] was copyrighted in 1926 by Max Ehrman. There is still controversy about which is the true story, yet its authorship does not detract from the truth and beauty of this piece.

Go placidly amid the noise and haste, and remember what peace there may be in silence. As far as possible, without surrender, be on good terms with all persons.

Speak your truth quietly and clearly; and listen to others, even to the dull and ignorant; they too have their story. Avoid loud and aggressive persons, they are vexations to the spirit.

---

35. "Things to be desired."

If you compare yourself with others, you may become vain and bitter, for always there will be greater and lesser persons than yourself.

Enjoy your achievements as well as your plans. Keep interested in your own career, however humble; it is a real possession in the changing fortunes of time.

Exercise caution in your business affairs, for the world is full of trickery. But let this not blind you to what virtue there is; many persons strive for high ideals, and everywhere life is full of heroism.

Be yourself. Especially do not feign affection. Neither be cynical about love; for in the face of all aridity and disenchantment it is as perennial as the grass. Take kindly the counsel of the years, gracefully surrendering the things of youth.

Nurture strength of spirit to shield you in sudden misfortune. But do not distress yourself with dark imaginings. Many fears are born of fatigue and loneliness.

Beyond a wholesome discipline, be gentle with yourself. You are a child of the universe no less than the trees and the stars; you have a right to be here. And whether or not it is clear to you, no doubt the universe is unfolding as it should.

Therefore be at peace with God, whatever you conceive Him to be. And whatever your labors and aspirations, in the noisy confusion of life, keep peace with your soul. With all its sham, drudgery and broken dreams, it is still a beautiful world.

Be cheerful. Strive to be happy.

BIBLIOGRAPHY

Berne, Eric: *Games People Play: The Psychology of Human Relations*. Grove Press, Inc. New York, 1964.

Cicero, Marcus Tullius: *Laelius; or, An Essay on Friendship*. General Books LLC, 2009.

Dickens, Charles: *David Copperfield*. Penguin Popular Classics, U.K., 1994.

Ellis, Bret Easton: *The Informers*. Picador, U.K., 1994.

Freud, Sigmund: *Obras Completas*. Editorial Biblioteca Nueva, Madrid, 1983.

Fromm, Erich: *The Art of Loving*. Harper Perennial Modern Classics, New York, 2006.

Graves, Robert: *The Greek Myths*. Penguin Books, Great Britain, 1980.

Harris, Thomas A.: *I'm OK—You're OK*. Avon Books, New York, 1973.

Hustvedt, Siri: *What I Loved*. Picador, New York, 2003.

James, Henry: *The Portrait of a Lady*. Bantam Books, New York, 1983.

Lacan, Jacques: *Écrits: A Selection*. W.W. Norton & Company, New York, 1977.

Laplanche , J. and Pontalis J.B.: *Diccionario de psicoanálisis*. Editorial Labor, Barcelona, 1981.

Lawrence, D.H.: *Women in Love*. Penguin Books, Great Britain, 1966.

——*Lady Chatterley's Lover*. Penguin Books, Great Britain, 1961.

Merajver-Kurlat, Marta: *Living with Stress.* Jorge Pinto
  Books Inc., New York, 2009.
Nin, Anaïs: *A Spy in the House of Love.* Bantam Books,
  New York, 1982.
Pahl, Raymond E.: *On Friendship.* Polity, U.K., 2000.
Plato: *Symposium.* Focus Publishing R. Pullins Company,
  U.S., 1998.
Proust, Marcel: *Swann's Way.* Viking, New York, 2003.
The Bible. http://www.bibleontheweb.com/Bible.asp
Shakespeare, William: *Hamlet.* Signet Classics, New
  York, 1963.
———*Othello.* Penguin Books, Great Britain, 1965.
Williams, Tennessee: *The Glass Menagerie.* Chelsea
  House, New York, 1988.
Yalom, Irvin D.: *Existential Psychotherapy.* Basic Books,
  Inc., New York, 1980.
———*The Schopenhauer Cure.* Harper Perennial, New
  York, 2006.

www.ingramcontent.com/pod-product-compliance
Lightning Source LLC
Chambersburg PA
CBHW031511270326
41930CB00006B/358